Sub Hunters

Maritime Patrol Aircraft – Ocean Surveillance – ASW Frigates – Homing Torpedoes

TOP: The Lockheed P-3C Orion was the classic sub hunter of the Cold War. (MARK WAGNER)

ABOVE: German U-boats almost brought Britain to its knees in World War Two. (US NAVY)

FAR LEFT: Nuclear-powered submarines can remain submerged almost indefinitely, making them hard to find and kill. (US NAVY)

LEFT: The mighty Merlin HM2 is the Royal Navy's main ASW helicopter. (MOD/CROWN COPYRIGHT VIA LEONARDO)

MAIN COVER IMAGE: More than 600 Lockheed P-3 Orions were built for the US Navy between 1960 and 1991. (LOCKHEED MARTIN)

ISBN: 978 1 80282 954 9
Editor: Tim Ripley
Data and photo research: Fergus Ripley
Senior editor, specials: Roger Mortimer
Email: roger.mortimer@keypublishing.com
Cover Design: Steve Donovan
Design: SJmagic DESIGN SERVICES, India
Advertising Sales Manager: Sam Clark
Email: sam.clark@keypublishing.com
Tel: 01780 755131

Advertising Production: Becky Antoniades
Email: Rebecca.antoniades@keypublishing.com

SUBSCRIPTION/MAIL ORDER
Key Publishing Ltd, PO Box 300, Stamford, Lincs, PE9 1NA
Tel: 01780 480404
Subscriptions email: subs@keypublishing.com

Mail Order email: orders@keypublishing.com
Website: www.keypublishing.com/shop

PUBLISHING
Group CEO and Publisher: Adrian Cox
Published by Key Publishing Ltd, PO Box 100, Stamford, Lincs, PE9 1XQ
Tel: 01780 755131
Website: www.keypublishing.com

PRINTING
Precision Colour Printing Ltd, Haldane, Halesfield 1, Telford, Shropshire. TF7 4QQ

DISTRIBUTION
Seymour Distribution Ltd, 2 Poultry Avenue, London, EC1A 9PU
Enquiries Line: 02074 294000.

The Sub Hunters

The Story of Anti-Submarine Warfare

The war against the submarine has taken many forms over the past century. In World War Two innovative tactics and new technology had to be brought to bear to defeat the German U-boat threat.

Then, during the 40 or so years of the Cold War, NATO's anti-submarine forces duelled their Soviet opponents in a shadow conflict that thankfully never turned into a real shooting war. And over the past decade tension with Russia and China have surged and the West has looked to bolstering its anti-submarine forces again.

In *Sub Hunters* we tell the story of how the war against the submarine has evolved. We look at the planes, helicopters, ships, and submarines that have been pitted against each other in this struggle for underwater supremacy.

The challenges in each of the major eras of submarine warfare are very different and we look at how the technology and tactics have changed over time.

While the duel between submarines and their hunters is at its heart a struggle for technological supremacy, it is also a human struggle. The machines involved had to be crewed. They spent days, weeks, or months enduring bad weather and extreme danger, all in the knowledge that at any moment they could face death or serious injury. Shipwrecked sailors cast adrift in the freezing North Atlantic only had a few hours life expectancy. There were few survivors from stricken U-boats.

Making the technology of sub hunting work is a challenge in itself. The need to gain an advantage over opponents, often meant new weapons or sensors had to be rushed into service so their crews would have little time to train to operate them before they would have to take them into battle. It was a case of training on the job. This required a can-do attitude and a willingness to take risks.

Despite a century's worth of technological development, personnel on sub hunting missions have to display the same essential skills. Hunting submarines – whether from the air, on the water or under the water - requires patience and the ability to piece together fragments of information collected during prolonged patrols, all while cold, wet, and tired. When their prey is discovered, they need to react instantly to strike and kill their opponent before it has a chance to escape.

We hope *Sub Hunters* is also a suitable tribute to the men and women who have fought in the great duel against submarines over the past century or so. The skills, expertise and bravery of anti-submarine forces is often overlooked compared the combat endeavours of fighter pilots, commandoes, or tank commanders.

Hunting submarines is a unique skillset and those who do it have a unique esprit de corps. In World War Two, Royal Air Force Coastal Command crews at first called themselves the 'Cinderella Command' because of their lower public profile compared to the 'glamour boys' of Fighter or Bomber Command. Then their more famous colleagues started to mock Coastal Command, dubbing it 'The Kipper Fleet'. Who actually coined the phrase is lost in time, but it is thought to refer to a jibe along the lines of, "all Coastal Command do is fish for kippers, while we in Fighter/Bomber Command are actually fighting and winning the war." In a typically British act of self deprecation, the Coastal Command crews - who knew better - turned the phrase around and started to call themselves The Kipper Fleet. It became a badge of honour and the name stuck. It remains in use today by the RAF maritime patrol personnel.

Tim Ripley
Editor
February 2024

ABOVE: The US Navy's P-8A Poseidon is the next generation of sub hunting aircraft.

LEFT: Tim Ripley meets the Mighty Hunter, circa 2010. (TIM RIPLEY)

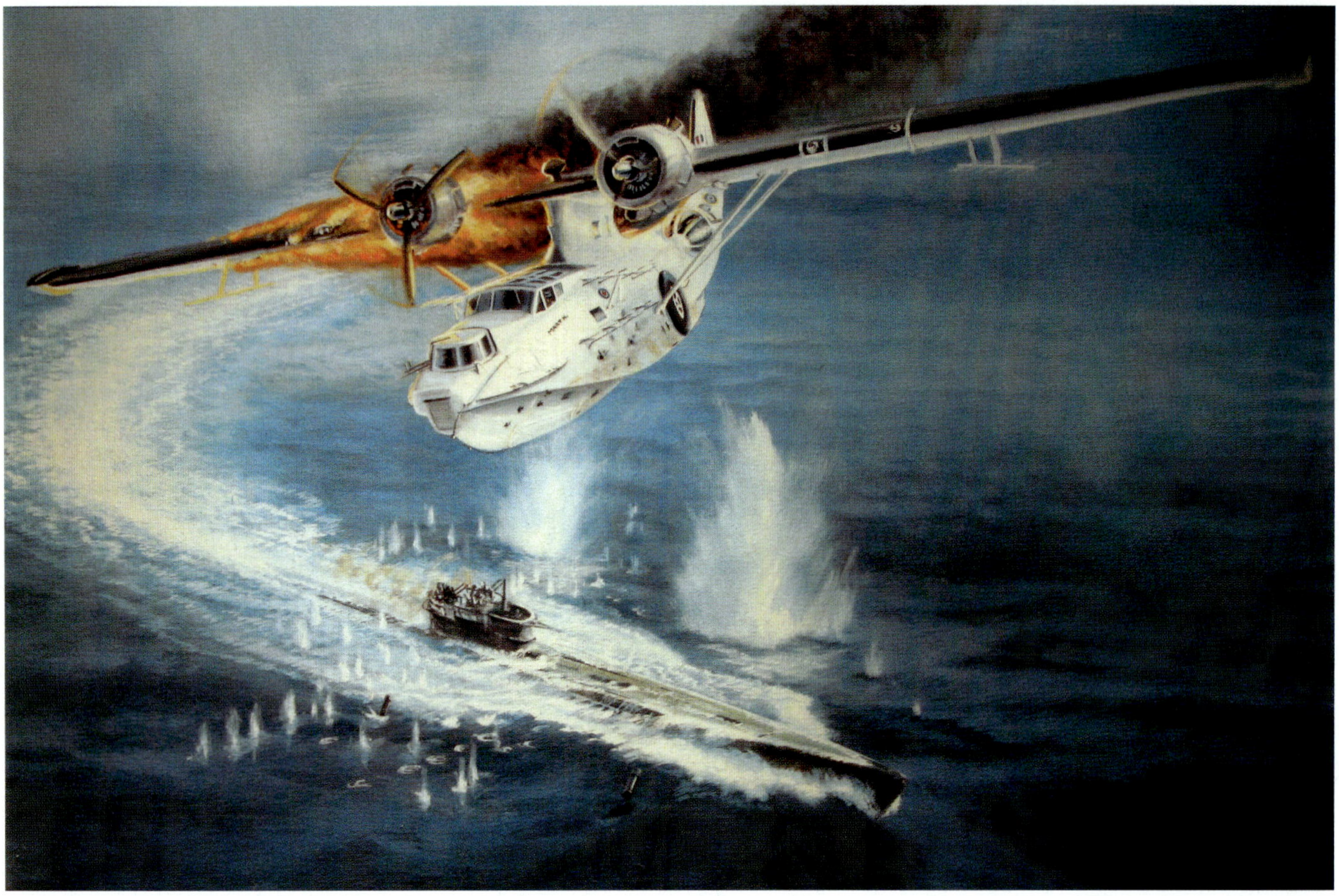

Killing Submarines

The Strategy and Tactics of Anti-Submarine Warfare

ABOVE: Royal Canadian Air Force Flight Lieutenant David Hornell's 'VC Attack'. Hornell and his crew successfully found and sank U-*1224* near the Faroe Islands. Their aircraft was badly damaged but Hornell managed to bring the flying boat down in a heavy swell. The crew survived for 21 hours in the single surviving dingy before being rescued. Hornell was the only RCAF flying boat pilot to win the British Empire's most prestigious medal for valour. (GRAHAM WRAGG, VIA CANADIA DEPARTMENT OF NATIONAL DEFENCE

Submarines are the ultimate silent killers. They approach their targets unseen and unheard. Hidden by the depths of the ocean, they strike their prey unawares before escaping to kill again.

Generations of sailors came to fear the submarines. Even the threat of their approach sent ship captains and crews into a panic, prompting them to stay in port, or turn around to seek safer waters.

Often the only warning that a ship was being targeted was when lookouts spotted inbound torpedoes from the tell-tale shape of their wake. Then it was too late. Seconds later the torpedoes would hit, ripping their target's hull apart and engulfing it in flames. The ship's crew would have only a few minutes to rush to the lifeboats or jump overboard to an uncertain fate, often in freezing water. Hours or days afloat in lifeboats or hanging on to wreckage would follow as shipwrecked sailors waited for rescue.

Submarines are the ultimate stealth weapon. The expanse of the world's oceans hides them from view, allowing them to cruise undetected over huge distance and then close with their targets. For more than a century, scientists, engineers, naval commanders, and aviators have all worked to try to find ways of countering the submarine threat.

RIGHT: U-*233* sinking after being rammed by USS *Thomas* in the North Atlantic on July 5, 1944, as photographed from the bridge of the US Navy destroyer. (US NATIONAL ARCHIVES)

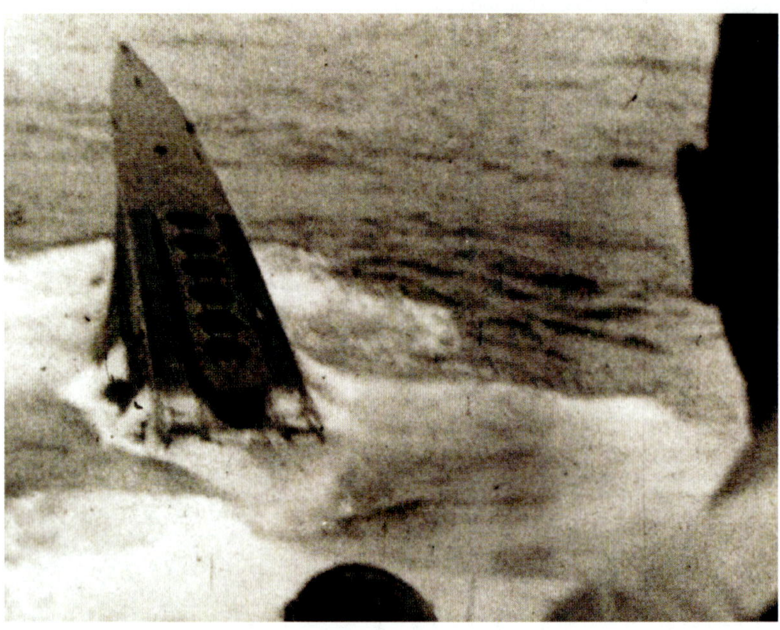

First, submarines must be detected and then tracked. Second, warships, aircraft or submarines have to be directed to the enemy submarines to positively identify them. And finally, they need to be provided with effective weapons to kill submarines cruising underwater.

Experience shows that winning against submarines requires a campaign approach that can be sustained over time. The struggle against submarines is a duel that involves move and then counter moves, as the enemy fields new technology, tactics, or strategies. How fast submarine hunters can react to new enemy moves can be the difference between victory or defeat.

The strategy of anti-submarine warfare is fundamentally driven by science and technology. Over the past 120 years of naval warfare, the development of submarine technology has driven how navies and air forces organise themselves to counter the threat. World War One era submarines could only remain submerged for an hour or so at the most so could be successfully countered by protecting merchant shipping with escort vessels.

By the time the Germans launched their U-boat campaign in the North Atlantic in World War Two, submarines could spend longer under water, but they still had to carry out long distance transits on the surface. The allies used this weakness to attack them when they were at their most vulnerable.

The arrival of nuclear power in the late 1950s transformed submarine warfare. Underwater detection technology had to be developed at a pace to monitor submarines that never had to surface, trying to pick up noise from them hundreds or thousands of kilometres away.

Submarines of the 21st century have reached new levels of performance that makes them even quieter and more difficult to detect.

The potential for technology to render submarines and anti-submarine weapons obsolete at a stroke means that investment in research and development is an essential element of a nation's sub hunting strategy. Probing weaknesses in enemies submarine technology can prove decisive, both tactically and strategically. New technology can provide a range of advantages, from marginal tactical benefits to decisive strategic developments. Nuclear powered submarines, for example, rendered the World War Two-era doctrine of anti-submarine warfare obsolete at a stroke. »

ABOVE: The P-3C Orion was the US Navy's primary anti-submarine aircraft of the Cold War. This aircraft is on final approach at Kadena Air Base in Okinawa, Japan in April 2019 - the Orion's final year in US Navy service. (BALON GREYJOY)

BELOW: U-*534* attempting to evade the attack of a RAF Coastal Command Liberator of 86 Squadron near Denmark. U-*534* was raised in 1993 and is on display at Birkenhead, near Liverpool. (AUSTRALIAN WAR MEMORIAL)

ABOVE: World War Two-era sub hunting crews worked in very noisy, cramped and uncomfortable conditions on board aircraft such as this Royal Canadian Air Force Shorts Sunderland. The endurance of the crews in such conditions had a major impact on their operational effectiveness. (CANADIAN MINISTRY NATIONAL DEFENCE)

and western anti-submarine secrets by recruiting a spy involved in the US Navy's top secret SOSUS underwater surveillance programme. This allowed the Soviets to build a new generation of super quiet submarines.

Building an operational-level plan to defeat an enemy submarine force is an art in itself. Naval and air force commanders have to marshal all their capabilities and then deploy them at the point of decisive effect. Unlike the great naval battles of old, individual submarines have to be killed one at a time, so anti-submarine campaign plans have to be built to sustain operations over months or years.

A good anti-submarine plan has to be able to access up-to-date and accurate intelligence of enemy submarine deployments and intentions. Then warships, submarines, and aircraft have to be employed to find and then kill the enemy submarines. A key element of anti-submarine planning can involve so-called asymmetric attacks, such as air attacks on enemy submarine bases or the construction yards where they are built.

Setting up a command-and-control structure that allows all elements of the anti-submarine force to operate together is at the heart of a successful submarine killing campaign. The role of intelligence was shown to be key, after the success of World War Two code breaking in the Battle of the Atlantic.

The allies won this intelligence battle, because they were able to pass

So, navies have gone to great lengths to protect the secrets of their submarines and gain access to their enemy's secrets. The turning point in the campaign against the U-boats in World War Two was the capture of German Enigma encoding machines and their cipher books. Knowing where U-boats were going to be and intercepting them was key to beating the 'wolfpacks'. At the height of the Cold War, the US Central Intelligence Agency even built a recovery ship specifically to lift the remains of a whole Soviet nuclear missile submarine that had sunk in the Pacific. The story could have been the plot line for a James Bond spy movie.

However, Soviet intelligence was also at work trying to gain insights into US

RIGHT: The modern sub-hunters onboard the Boeing P-8A Poseidon work in very different conditions to their World War Two counterparts and have access to huge amount of intelligence data via satellite communication links. (US NAVY)

German Enigma secrets rapidly to naval commanders so they could try to re-route convoys away from U-boat wolf packs.

Good intelligence might be able to pinpoint the position of an enemy submarine, but actually killing it is not a foregone conclusion. To put a weapon on target to kill a submarine is never easy. Even the best modern underwater technology only provides a fleeting contact with enemy submarines. So, submarine hunters have to spend time trying to localise confused information to pinpoint the exact position of their target. It takes skilled operators and commanders to know when they have their prey trapped. Often this requires split second reactions, to engage a target as soon as it comes into view.

Anti-submarine commanders are also aware that at any moment, their prey could turn the tables and strike back. A skilled enemy submarine captain will try to dodge detection until the point at which they can become the hunter.

Both the hunter and the hunted know that a single mistake could doom them to destruction and their crews to certain death. Few submarine crews survive if their boat is destroyed or seriously damaged while submerged. Modern warships are not designed to take heavy damage, so a hit from torpedo is likely to result in them sinking quickly with major loss of life.

Despite modern submarine hunting being portrayed as a duel by hi-tech forces and remotely launched weapons, the human element remains central. Crews of warships in the North Atlantic still have to battle mountainous waves and freezing seas. Maritime patrol aircraft crews have spent hours circling over stormy seas and must react at a moment's notice to fleeting contacts with the enemy. Under the waves, submariners have to await their fate knowing that in a split second their vessel could be destroyed, dooming them to a watery fate with little means of escape.

LEFT: Royal Air Force Poseidon anti-submarine aircraft are to be equipped with the BAE System Stingray homing torpedo to enhance their sub-killing arsenal. (MOD CROWN COPYRIGHT)

BELOW: Dipping sonar is a potent and effective way for anti-submarine helicopters to find their prey. (US NAVY)

Dawn of Submarine Warfare

First Battles against Submarines

The Confederate submarine *H. L. Hunley* made history by being the first submarine to successfully sink an enemy warship. (CONRAD WISE CHAPMAN/AMERICAN CIVIL WAR MUSEUM)

The first recorded sinking of a ship by a submarine took place off Charleston harbour on February 17, 1864, during the American Civil War. In a bid to break the Union blockade of the port, the Confederate submarine *H. L. Hunley* rammed her spar or bow torpedo into USS *Housatonic*'s starboard side. The crew of the Union sloop briefly saw the submarine as it rammed into the side of their ship and attached its explosive torpedo.

The explosion blasted a hole in the USS *Housatonic*'s hull and within five minutes she was underwater. Most of her crew survived by climbing up her masts as the ship settled on the sea bed. However, the crew of the *H. L. Hunley* did not live to see their success. The underwater blast damaged the submarine, and she sank with all hands.

Despite the 'backfire' the episode convinced many navies that submarines could be effective weapons of war and by the outbreak of World War One, most European navies had dozens of the vessels in service. The French had 123, Russia

The *H. L. Hunley* was recovered from Charleston Harbor in August 2000, and it was discovered that she had been sunk by the explosion of her own torpedo. (BARBARA VOULGARIS, NAVAL HISTORICAL CENTER - NAVAL HISTORICAL CENTER)

had 41, Italy 25, and the British had 57, but 40 of these were suitable only to serve in coastal waters. Germany bought it first submarine in 1906 and it had 30 ready for action when World War One broke out in 1914. These were dubbed 'unterseeboot' in German but were quickly nicknamed U-boats. The name spread fear among Allied sailors in two world wars.

The next four years saw the first widespread use of submarines and the development of tactics and equipment to defeat them. World War One era submarines had very limited ability to operate underwater and could only remain submerged for a couple of hours at most. This meant most engagements between warships and submarines took place on the surface.

First blood in World War One fell to the Royal Navy cruiser, HMS *Birmingham* in August 1914. The British warship discovered a U-boat on the surface in the North Sea as its crews were trying to make repairs and was able to ram and sink the submarine.

A month later, U-*21*, commanded by Lieutenant Otto Hersing, made history when it torpedoed the Royal Navy light cruiser HMS *Pathfinder* in the North Sea. The cruiser's magazine exploded, and the ship sank in four minutes, taking 259 of her crew with her. It was the first combat victory of a modern submarine.

The German navy moved to expand the size of its U-boat fleet to launch a campaign to isolate Britain by sinking merchant ships carrying vital war equipment and raw materials. At first the U-boats surfaced to attack merchant vessels and give their crews time to abandon ship before opening fire. However, within weeks the German U-boats began opening fire without warning to start what became known as their campaign of unrestricted submarine warfare.

To try to bring down losses, the Royal Navy began organising merchant ships into convoys and provide them with escorts. This resulted in a dramatic drop in ship losses.

In a bid to trick U-boats into exposing themselves, the Royal Navy began fitting out merchant ships with concealed guns, which it dubbed Q-ships. These pretended to be isolated merchant ships and if a U-boat took the bait and surfaced to attack, the crew would uncover their guns and engage the submarine.

As German submarine technology improved, the British looked to devise technologies to attack them underwater. The Royal Navy developed the first hydrophones to listen for underwater submarines and these became the first sonar. At the time this was dubbed ASDIC after the Anti-Submarine Detection Investigation Committee that had ordered its development. Warships were equipped with bombs that detonated at a pre-set depth to create what became known as depth charges.

German submarines eventually sank more than eight million tons of allied merchant shipping and caused major problems for the British war economy. The introduction of convoys and Q-ships reduced allied losses, eventually leading to the sinking of more than 150 U-boats out of 350 built during the war. However, the campaign of unrestricted submarine warfare backfired on Germany. When the campaign was expanded to include neutral shipping in January 1917, it significantly contributed to the decision by the United States to declare war on Germany three months later.

TOP: German U-boats proved to be deadly opponents during World War One and convinced many navies of the future utility of the submarine in naval warfare. (IMPERIAL WAR MUSEUM)

ABOVE: Early German U-boats had many technical limitations, and it was only after World War One that these were successfully overcome. (PRIVATE COLLECTION)

The U-boat Threat

Germany's Submarine Force in World War Two

ABOVE: A German U-boat comes under depth charge attack in the North Atlantic. Its gun crews are engaging Allied patrol aircraft. U-boats rarely won these engagements thanks to the determination of the Allied aircrews to press home their attacks.
(AUSTRALIAN WAR MEMORIAL)

RIGHT: Captured German U-boats outside their pen at Trondheim in Norway in May 1945. These Type VII and a Type IX submarines were the stalwarts of the U-boat force during the Battle of the Atlantic.
(IMPERIAL WAR MUSEUM)

The attack – only seven weeks into the war – had a major impact back in Berlin. Germany's navy had only begun building submarines six years earlier when Adolf Hitler had come to power and repudiated the hated Treaty of Versailles that had banned Germany from building and operating submarines. Hitler launched a secret programme to restart submarine production and set up its U-boat arm, but the senior leadership of the German navy were convinced their surface fleet, not U-boats, would be decisive in any war with the British.

Hitler publicly broke with Versailles in 1935 and renamed his navy the *Kriegsmarine*. The U-boat arm was now set up and Captain Karl Dönitz was placed in charge of the 1st U-boat Flotilla. By the start of the war in 1939, Dönitz was the head of the German U-boat command, or BdU. He moulded the U-boat arm in his image, and he was idolised by submarine crews, as 'the Lion'.

Prien's attack on Scapa Flow proved pivotal to the U-boat force. When the daring captain returned his boat to Germany, he and his crew were immediately flown to Berlin to be

In the early hours of October 15, 1939, the reborn German U-boat fleet showed what it could do. U-47's captain, Günther Prien, navigated his boat on the surface through a narrow waterway to enter Scapa Flow, the supposedly secure anchorage of the British fleet in the heart of the Orkney archipelago.

Prien then manoeuvred his boat into a firing position close to battleship, HMS *Royal Oak*, and fired a salvo of torpedoes at the Royal Navy vessel as most its crew slept. When he judged his first torpedoes had missed, Prien calmly ordered his crew to reload the boat's forward tubes. Second time lucky, the torpedoes hit home and engulfed HMS *Royal Oak* in flames. In only 13 minutes, the battleship went to the bottom of Scapa Flow and took 835 crew with her. Now Prien made his escape, again on the surface he navigated U-47 out of Scapa Flow and into the North Sea. In a matter of minutes, the U-boat force had struck a devastating blow against the Royal Navy and left the Admiralty in London reeling.

U-BOAT LOSSES, 1939 TO 1945	
Year	Losses
1939	9
1940	24
1941	35
1942	87
1943	244
1944	249
1945	120
Total	768

LEFT: The commander of the U-boat force, Karl Dönitz, was known as 'The Lion' by his crews because of his determination to prove that submarines alone could defeat Britain and the Royal Navy. (BUNDESARCHIV)

personally decorated by Hitler. The U-boat captain was awarded the Knights Cross, Germany's highest gallantry decoration, and all the crew received the Iron Cross. Hitler was suddenly excited by U-boats and Dönitz started to find his ideas to build a 300 strong fleet of submarines to strangle Britain's maritime trade were looked on favourably by the German navy high command. He was given the authority to build up his U-boats into the powerful force that brought the British to the brink of defeat in the Battle of the Atlantic within three years.

Although the Nazi propaganda machine feted the U-boat force, it was far from being a creation of Hitler's political regime. Its commander, Dönitz, had briefly been a U-boat captain in World War One. His boat had been sunk during a battle with a British warship in 1918 and he spent the rest of the war in a prison camp. As a result, he had a visceral hatred of all things British and, in particular, the Royal Navy. He was convinced »

LEFT: The U-boat pens at Saint-Nazaire were built with reinforced concrete roofs to protect the vital submarines from Allied bombers. They survived the war and today house a museum. (KATEZNIK)

BELOW: U-534 was sunk off Denmark in May 1945 after refusing to surrender at the end of World War Two. The submarine was subsequently salvaged and is now on display at Birkenhead on Merseyside. (PAUL ADAMS)

RIGHT: Complete sections, comprising the pressure hull with outer skin, of a Type XXI U-boat are brought together in a German shipyard in 1944. (PRIVATE COLLECTION)

BELOW: U-*3008* was one of four highly advanced Type XXI submarines that were ready for action in May 1945. She sported an advanced snorkel system to allow her to operate almost totally underwater throughout a war cruise. The US Navy took control of the submarine after the war to study her advanced technology. (US NAVY)

ALLIED MERCHANT LOSSES TO U-BOATS, 1939 TO 1945	
Country	Ships hit
British	1,660
American	549
Norwegian	314
Dutch	137
Greek	124
Total	2,784

that a new generation of U-boats, with greater range, better torpedoes and improved batteries that allowed them to submerge for several hours would enable the *Kriegsmarine* to break the Royal Navy's convoys.

His first move was to accelerate the production of the long-range U-boats that could range far out into the Atlantic. The German ship building industry ramped up U-boat production and introduced new construction methods. This included block assembly techniques, so hundreds could be built each year. In September 1939 only 26 U-boats were fit to go to sea out of fleet of 41. U-boat production was surged to replace losses in the first years of the war. So, by early 1943, the *Kriegsmarine* boasted 240 U-boats, of which 112 were operational in the North Atlantic.

To command the U-boat offensive, Dönitz set up a centralised control system to direct each submarine to specific operating areas. He linked his U-boat command to the code breaking and radio direction finding

ABOVE: U-995 is preserved as a memorial to all mariners lost in conflict at the Naval Museum in Laboe near Kiel, Germany. (DARKONE)

organisation, the *B-Dienst*, which scored major successes in breaking Royal Navy communications.

Once intelligence had found a British convoy, U-boats were directed by radio messages to attack them. Dönitz expected his captains to regularly radio back sightings of British ships and weather reports to allow further attacks to be planned. The North Atlantic was divided into a series of grid squares to speed up changes in plans.

By 1943, the U-boats were hunting in large groups, known as wolf packs, to sink Allied merchant ships heading for British ports loaded with vital food, raw materials, and arms to keep Britain fighting. More than a dozen U-boats were massed for wolf pack attacks on convoys at the height of the Battle of the Atlantic in 1942 and early 1943.

Dönitz's centralised control of the U-boat fleet turned it into a potent force, but it also created a critical vulnerability. The British code-breaking organisation at Bletchley Park was regularly able to break the Enigma code used by the U-boats and this revealed Dönitz's innermost secrets to his enemies.

Despite many of the advances incorporated in U-boat designs early in the war, Dönitz's fleet also had some important vulnerabilities. U-boats had to spend a long time on the surface re-charging their batteries and refilling their air banks, transmitting/receiving radio messages, or transferring supplies from so-called 'mother' submarines. In the first three years of the war, U-boats were able to operate on the surface in the centre of the North Atlantic without risk of attack and so could mass to track convoys. They could save their precious air and battery power for the close quarter attacks. Many U-boat captains felt so confident they would even attack convoys on the surface. However, it meant during their long transit from bases in western France, Norway, and Germany, U-boats had to cruise on the surface opening them up to detection and attack from the air.

To close this vulnerability, Dönitz ordered the development of U-boats equipped with snorkels which were a Dutch invention that had been seized when German troops captured the Netherlands in 1940. This was an exhaust pipe that could be raised while a U-boat was submerged to allow it to run its diesel engine while expelling carbon monoxide from the vessel. Fortunately for the Allies, snorkel equipped U-boats were not available in large numbers before the end of the war.

U-boat captains and their crews were highly motivated professionals, who knew their trade and pressed home their attacks with great determination. They were the elite of the *Kriegsmarine* and were routinely lauded in Nazi propaganda. However, no amount of bravery could compensate for the superiority of Allied anti-submarine technology and tactics that progressively stripped away the advantages of the U-boats as the war progressed.

BELOW: U-boat U-617 was run aground near Melilla off the Spanish coast by RAF Wellington bombers from 179 Squadron on September 12, 1943. All crew members were able to evacuate the stricken submarine and subsequently interned by the Spanish authorities. The wreck was destroyed by gunfire from the Allied warships, HMS *Hyacinth*, and HMAS *Wollongong*. (IMPERIAL WAR MUSEUM)

Allied Anti-Submarine Strategy

Defeating the U-Boats

ABOVE: The US tanker, *Dixie Arrow*, was torpedoed of the coast of North Carolina by *U-71* in March 1942 when German submarines ran amok along the east coast of America until a convoy system was enacted by the US Navy. (IMPERIAL WAR MUSEUM)

In September 1939, Britain was poorly placed to deal with the threat of the U-boats. The Royal Navy and Royal Air Force did not have escort ships or maritime patrol aircraft with the range to operate in the centre of the North Atlantic. This critical region became known as the Gap'. Here U-boats could operate on the surface with impunity and hundreds of Allied merchant ships were sunk as a result.

Late in 1939, the decision was taken that merchant ships must sail across the Atlantic in convoys under naval escort, which did much to help stem losses. A key advantage was the Ultra code breaking organisation at Bletchley Park whose successes allowed the Admiralty to track in real-time the U-boats' movements. This allowed convoys to be routed away from wolf packs. Despite these advantages, merchant shipping losses continued to rise and in 1942 more than 650,000 tons of merchant shipping was sunk by U-boats.

It was clear to the Admiralty that a major revamp of the war against the U-boats was needed. Orders were placed for new escort ships and maritime patrol aircraft to close 'the Gap' but these would take time to be delivered. Britain's naval chiefs also realised that the whole campaign had to be re-organised, better co-ordination set up between the RAF and RN, and with intelligence distribution streamlined. Anti-submarine forces needed to be trained to fight together as dedicated units to maximise the effectiveness of new technology.

To run the convoy battles, in the summer of 1940 a dedicated combined headquarters was set up, originally in Plymouth and, from February 1941, at Derby House in Liverpool. It was named Headquarters Western Approaches and soon became the hub of all British naval and air operations against the U-boats. The headquarters of RAF Coastal Command's 15 Group was also re-located to Derby House to fully integrate maritime patrol aircraft

RIGHT: The main plotting room at Derby House in Liverpool was the nerve centre of Headquarters Western Approaches at the peak of the Battle of the Atlantic. (TIM RIPLEY)

operations with the convoys they were escorting.

Under the leadership of Admiral Sir Percy Noble and then Admiral Max Horton, the plotting room in Derby House kept track of every convoy and maritime patrol aircraft searching for U-boats in the North Atlantic. Life and death decisions were made in this room as the admirals and their staff considered the progress of the battle.

However, good staff work alone was not enough to defeat the U-boats, so Headquarters Western Approaches set up its own training units in Liverpool, Londonderry, and Greenock to prepare escort groups for convoy duty. A dedicated Anti-Submarine Training School, dubbed HMS *Western Isles*, was set up in Tobermory on the west coast of Scotland to train up every Royal Navy escort ship's company before they headed out to take on the U-boats.

Adm Horton is credited with moving the convoy battle up a gear and bringing in several tactical innovations. He was instrumental in forming dedicated escort and support groups, which transformed how convoys fought off U-boats. He also started deploying rescue ships in convoys to pick up sunken sailors, so escort ships could continue with fighting off the U-boats.

And, at the same time as the Royal Navy and RAF were beefing up Headquarters Western Approaches, a similar organisation was established in Canada to run the campaign against the U-boats in the North West Atlantic. Along with the Royal Canadian Air Force, the Royal Canadian Navy role was instrumental in creating a joined up anti-submarine campaign plan for the whole of the North Atlantic.

The United States played a secondary role in the Battle of the Atlantic because of the US Navy's stance that the Pacific theatre was their priority. However, some US Navy and US Army Air Forces patrol aircraft did deploy to Iceland and Britain from 1942 under British direction. Escort ships from the US Navy and US Coast Guard also operated in the North Atlantic but not on the same scale as British and Canadian vessels.

ABOVE: Royal Navy officers on the bridge of an escort vessel keep a look out for enemy submarines during the Battle of the Atlantic in October 1941. (IMPERIAL WAR MUSEUM)

LEFT: Headquarters Western Approaches in Liverpool is preserved as a museum, and it provides an unrivalled insight into the Battle of the Atlantic. (TIM RIPLEY)

Allied Maritime Patrol Aircraft

The Battle of the Atlantic saw the first development of dedicated anti-submarine warfare, or ASW, aircraft to defeat the U-boats.

The need for U-boats to operate on the surface to move rapidly to their patrol areas or in order to recharge their batteries meant that the German submarines had a crucial vulnerability. Long range maritime patrol aircraft were well placed to strike at U-boats on the surface, particularly in the region of the North Atlantic known as 'the Gap'.

Leading the air war against the U-boats was RAF Coastal Command, which before World War Two had operated a fleet of flying boats to monitor enemy naval activity, as well as carry out rescues.

At the beginning of the war in 1939 Coastal Command had 39 Short Sunderland flying boats and they were soon escorting convoys in British home waters. They scored several kills of U-boats using their heavy machine guns, mounted in their forward gun turrets. To supplement the fleet, dozens of Lockheed Hudsons were bought from America to patrol in coastal regions.

By 1942, long range American-supplied Consolidated B-24 Liberator bombers, Boeing B-17 Flying Fortress and Consolidated PBY Catalina flying boats were arriving to allow Coastal Command to spread its wings further out into the Atlantic. New bases had been opened in Iceland, the Azores and in Northern Ireland to bring more of 'the Gap' within range. Then, when the US entered the war in December 1941, US Navy and US Army Air Forces patrol squadrons began heading out over the Atlantic to help RAF Coastal Command.

Extraordinary efforts were put into finding bases to close 'the Gap' including opening a flying boat base on Lough Erne in Country Fermanagh in Northern Ireland. The United States opened a secret back channel to the neutral government of the Irish Republic to allow British and Canadian flying boats to briefly fly through Irish airspace, saving vital flying time and fuel. US Navy instructors were sent to Fermanagh to teach the British and Canadian crews to fly newly delivered Catalinas, so the neutral Irish felt obliged to help out its American 'friends'. Powerful Irish-American politicians played an important part in influencing the staunchly neutral government in Dublin to turn a blind eye to the flights from Loch Erne.

During 1942 and into 1943, RAF experimental units were working hard to field specialist technology to help the Coastal Command crews find and kill U-boats. The biggest boost was the installation of

surveillance radars which allowed the RAF crews to detect U-boats on the surface at night and at long range. This was complemented by the fitting of steerable search lights - known as Leigh Lights - which helped gunners in patrol aircraft to find U-boats at night. A further development on US aircraft was the installation of magnetic anomaly detector, or MAD, booms which set off alerts when they overflew a large metal object, such as a submarine.

Once they had found an enemy submarine, the patrol aircraft could move in for the kill with their machine guns and depth charges. After U-boats were fitted with bigger 88mm anti-aircraft guns, the Allies reacted by up-gunning their patrol aircraft with bigger calibre weapons.

RAF and Allied sub-hunting crews soon learned that they only had a brief window to attack after sighting a submarine on the surface. If they did not strike quickly, the U-boat would crash dive and escape. As soon as a U-boat was sighted, the aircraft captain would point the nose of his aircraft at the submarine and dive at full speed. The nose gunner would immediately open fire to rake the U-boat, hopefully killing the conning tower crew and punching holes in the hull, to make it dangerous to submerge. When the attacking aircraft was over the U-boat, the pilot would pull up and release a stick of bombs or depth charges. If they landed on target this would devastate the U-boat. Such attacks required nerves of steel to dive into hails of German machine gun fire. Not surprisingly, many RAF Coastal Command pilots were highly decorated, with three receiving the Victoria Cross for pressing home attacks against U-boats.

By the summer of 1943, there were enough patrol aircraft to fully cover 'the Gap in daylight hours. Nowhere was to be safe for U-boats to operate undetected from the air.

RAF AND ALLIED MARITIME PATROL AIRCRAFT UNITS, FEBRUARY 1943		
Unit	Aircraft	Location
Royal Air Force Coastal Command		
18 Group, RAF		Rosyth, Scotland
190 Squadron, RAF	6 x Catalina	Sullom Voe, Shetland
612 Squadron, RAF	16 x Wellington	Wick, Scotland
15 Group, RAF		Derby House, Liverpool
330 Squadron, Royal Norwegian Air Force	6 x N-3PB Nomad	Reykjavík, Iceland
VP-84, US Navy	12 x Catalina	Reykjavík, Iceland
120 Squadron RAF (part)	6 x Liberators	Reykjavík, Iceland
269 Squadron, RAF	20 x Hudson	Kaldadrenes, Iceland
206 Squadron, RAF	9 x B-17	Benbecula, Scotland
246 Squadron, RAF	6 x Sunderland	Bowmore, Scotland
120 Squadron, RAF (part)	16 x Liberator	Ballykelly, Northern Ireland
220 Squadron, RAF	9 x B-17	Ballykelly, Northern Ireland
201 Squadron, RAF	6 x Sunderland	Castle Archdale, Northern Ireland
423 Squadron, Royal Canadian Air Force	6 x Sunderland	Castle Archdale, Northern Ireland
228 Squadron, RAF	6 x Sunderland	Castle Archdale, Northern Ireland
19 Group, RAF		Mountbatten, Devon
311 Squadron, Free Czech Air Force	16 x Wellignton	Talbenny, Wales
304 Suadron, Free Polish Air Force	16 x Wellignton	Dale, Wales
210 Squadron, RAF	6 x Catalina	Pembroke Dock, Wales
172 Squadron, RAF	16 x Wellignton	Chivenor, Cornwall
59 Squadron, RAF	9 x B-17	Chivenor, Cornwall
No 10 OTU, RAF (loaned by Bomber Command)	20 x Whitney	St Eval, Cornwall
502 Squadron, RAF	16 x Whitney	St Eval, Cornwall
1st Anti-Submarine Squadron, US Army Air Force	12 x Liberator	St Eval, Cornwall
2nd Anti-Submarine Squadron, US Army Air Force	12 x Liberator	St Eval, Cornwall
10 Squadron, Royal Australian Air Force	6 x Sunderland	Mountbatten, Devon
Royal Canadian Air Force - Eastern Air Command		**Halifax, Nova Scotia**
5 Squadron, RCAF	Canso (Catalina)	RCAF Station Gander
10 Squadron, RCAF	Douglas Digby	RCAF Station Yarmouth
11 Squadron, RCAF	PBY Catalina	RCAF Station Dartmouth
113 Squadron, RCAF	Hudson	RCAF Station Yarmouth
116 Squadron, RCAF	PBY Catalina	RCAF Station Dartmouth
117 Squadron, RCAF	Canso (Catalina)	RCAF Station Dartmouth
119 Squadron, RCAF	Hudson	RCAF Station Sydney

ABOVE: RAF Coastal Command Sunderland flying boats of 201 Squadron operated from Castle Archdale on the banks of Lough Erne in Northern Ireland to close 'the Gap' in the middle of the North Atlantic. (IMPERIAL WAR MUSEUM)

ABOVE: At its peak, more than 30 Sunderland and Catalina flying boats were stationed at Castle Archdale Northern Ireland, flown by British, Canadian, and US crews. When Lough Erne froze in January 1945 the flying boats had to be taken out of the water. (IMPERIAL WAR MUSEUM)

Battle of the Codes

Code Breaking and the U-boat War

RIGHT: The four rotor German Navy Enigma machine proved extremely difficult to crack for several months at the height of the Battle of the Atlantic. This one is on display at Bletchley Park museum.
(MAGNUS MANSKE)

FAR RIGHT: A sample of decryption from Bletchley Park. A first draft extracted key words from the original German message, and they had to be further analysed by language and military experts to identify more information.
(DR DAVID HAMER/USAF)

BELOW: After *U-110* was forced to the surface by HMS *Bulldog*, *Broadway*, and *Arbretia* northwest of Ireland in May 1941, a Royal Navy boarding party successfully recovered an Enigma machine and code books giving Bletchley Park a crucial advance in the 'Battle of the Codes'. The incident provided the inspiration for the Hollywood movie, *U-571*, but with US Navy sailors portrayed as having captured the vital encoding machine.
(IMPERIAL WAR MUSEUM)

The U-boat chief Karl Dönitz created a complex command and control network to control his submarine fleet, via radio. This was the first time that a naval campaign had been run in such a centralised way.

From his headquarters in a French Chateau, Dönitz was able to pull together intelligence from his highly efficient code breaking and radio direction finding organisation, the B-Dienst, as well as sighting reports from U-boats and Luftwaffe Focke-Wulf Fw 200 Condor long range patrol aircraft.

But alongside the efficiency there was also a crucial weakness in Dönitz's command system. The British code breakers at Bletchley Park, who used the codename Ultra, had worked out how to crack the Enigma encoding machines used by all branches of the German military,

including the U-boat fleet. This used three electronic wheels to encode and decode text. By 1941 the British were routinely reading a large part of German radio traffic thanks to the world's first computer that was able to work through the combination of possible letters used by the Enigma machine.

The German high command was largely blissfully unaware that Enigma had been broken and continued to use it to send top secret information. German navy communications experts were more cautious about the security of Enigma. In February 1942, the Kriegsmarine introduced machines fitted with a fourth wheel for use by the U-boat fleet, which at a stroke made it impossible for the British to read the communications of the U-boat fleet. For nine months, Royal Navy intelligence lost key insights into U-boat operations and the situation was only restored after a German code-book was seized from a sinking U-boat, U-559, after a party of Royal Navy sailors boarded her.

To support the Bletchley Park code breakers, the Royal Navy also built up a network of direction-finding stations in Britain and around the North Atlantic to pinpoint the location of U-boats from their radio transmissions. So even though for many months in 1942 the British could not read U-boat radio traffic, they were still able to triangulate the position of most of Dönitz's U-boat fleet.

Enigma was a key advantage for the Allies in the Battle of the Atlantic and it allowed the Royal Navy to re-route many convoys away from wolf packs, strike at U-boats transiting to operational areas, and understand the order of battle of the U-boat fleet.

The code-breaking war was not completely one sided. Dönitz's B-Dienst intelligence agency successfully broke Royal Navy codes for much of the first three years of the war. This allowed the U-boat chief to track convoys and mass his wolf packs to best effect. From December 1942 to May 1943, 80% of Royal Navy radio messages were intercepted and read by the Germans, but they lacked an efficient analysis and distribution system so only 10% of them were decrypted in time to take effective action. B-Dienst also broke the US Navy's codes in 1942 and this helped the U-boats run amok along the eastern seaboard of the United States in early 1942. Towards the end of 1943, the British and US navies introduced new encoding machines and the B-Dienst lost its advantage for the remainder of the war.

The role of code breaking in the Battle of the Atlantic showed the importance of intelligence into planning anti-submarines operations. In the Cold War, the British and Americans sought to devise new technologies to give them a decisive edge over the Soviet submarine fleet.

ABOVE: The Colossus Mark 2 computer transformed the ability of Bletchley Park code breakers to crack the Enigma.
(IMPERIAL WAR MUSEUM)

LEFT: The British Admiralty introduced the Cypher No. 5 code book in June 1943, and this thwarted B-Dienst efforts to crack Royal Navy codes.
(IMPERIAL WAR MUSEUM)

Short Sunderland

The Flying Porcupine

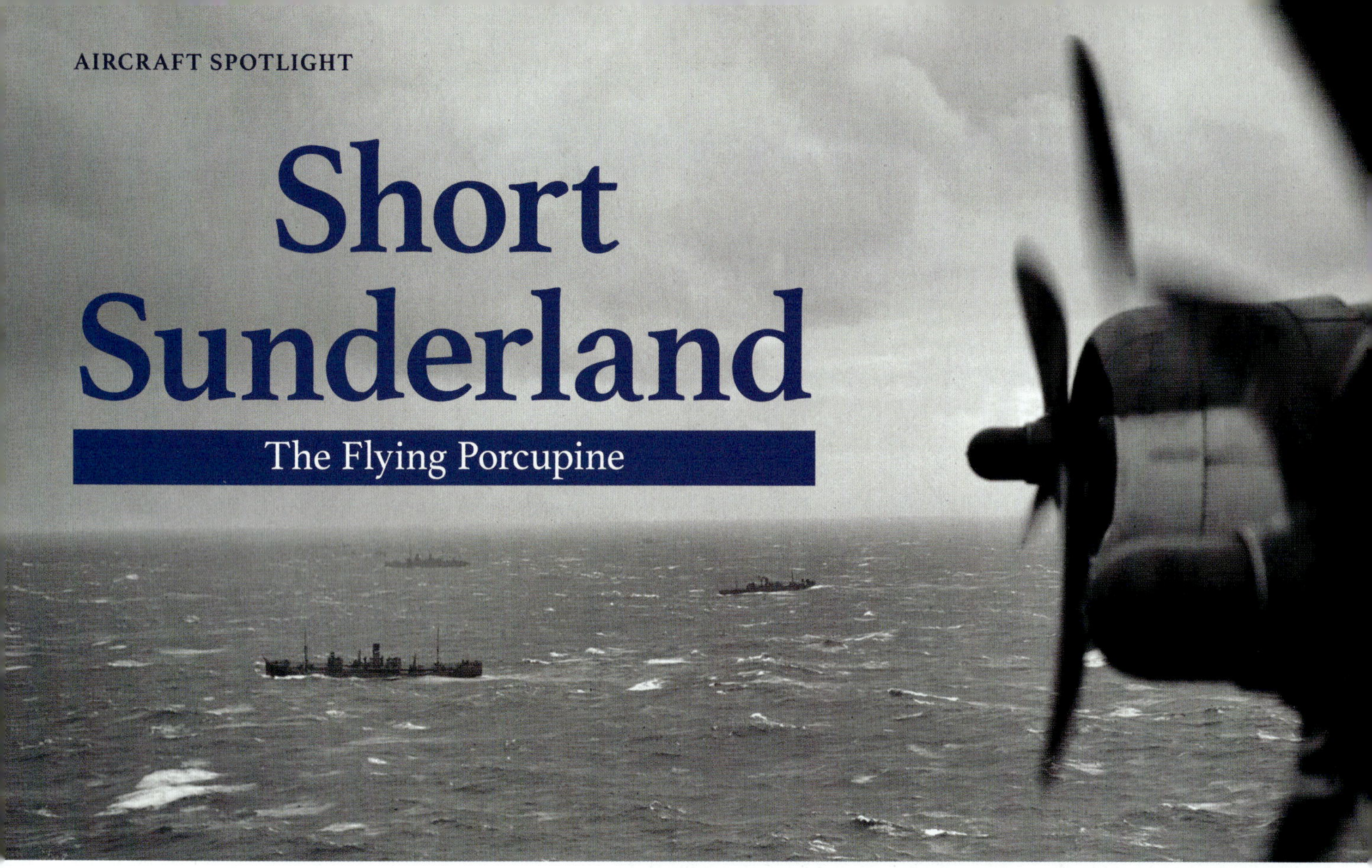

ABOVE: Sunderland crews provided overwatch for North Atlantic convoys, forcing U-boats to remain submerged and limiting their ability to recharge their batteries. (IMPERIAL WAR MUSEUM)

The classic British maritime patrol aircraft of World War Two was developed as the military variant of the Short Brothers' S23 Empire civilian passenger flying boat.

By the time production ceased in 1946, some 777 Sunderland patrol variants had been built for the Royal Air Force and Allied air arms. Crews from Australia, New Zealand, and Canada joined RAF Coastal Command Sunderland squadrons flying missions against the U-boats for the duration of the Battle of the Atlantic. They built bonds that remain to this day in the shape of the Fincastle Trophy that tests the skills of Commonwealth maritime patrol crews.

The flying boat's distinctive shape and internal configuration owed at lot to pre-war clippers that were designed to provide luxury global travel for high wealth individuals.

When the first military variant, the Sunderland took to the skies in 1937 it boasted nose, dorsal and tail rotating gun turrets, which each had twin .303 machine guns. Waist guns added to the aircraft's impressive firepower and bombs, or depth charges were carried internally and then moved into position under aircraft wings by a mechanical hoist system.

The aircraft interior was configured with sleeping bunks so extra-personnel could be carried to help bolster the endurance of the flight crew.

The RAF had originally ordered the Sunderland to police Britain's

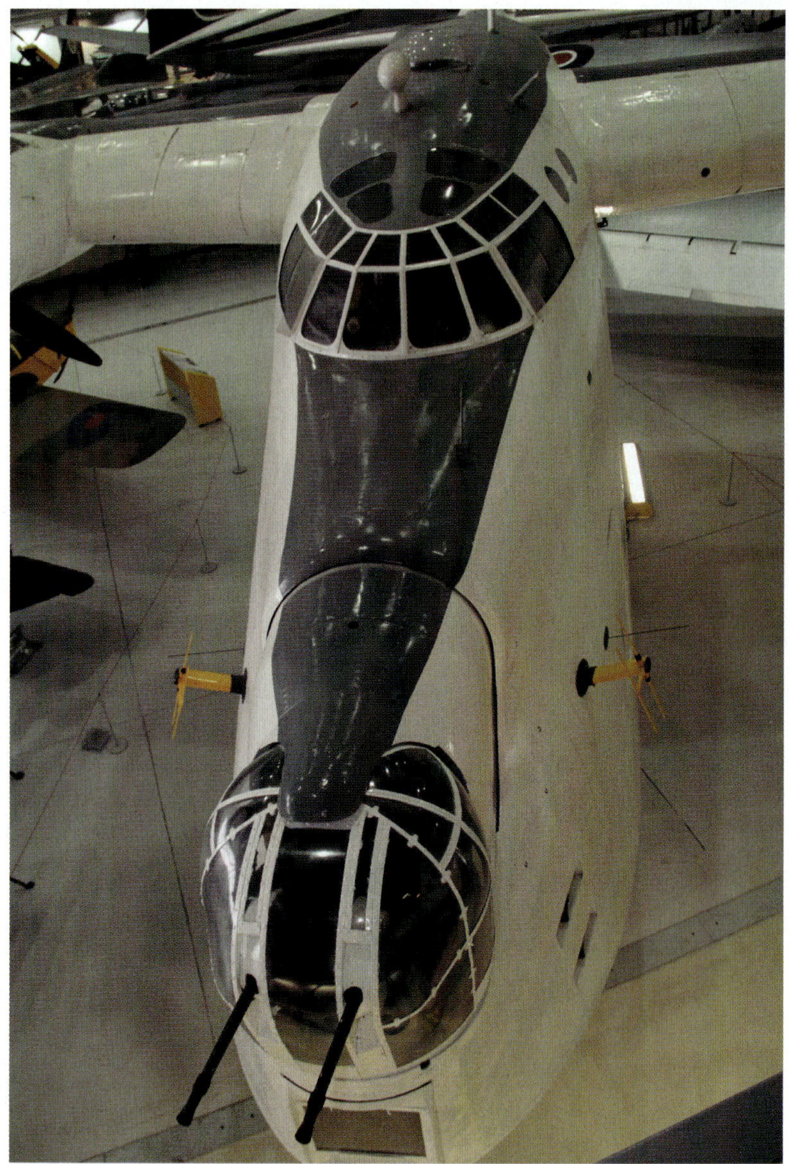

RIGHT: The Sunderland was dubbed the 'Flying Porcupine' by U-boat crews because of its heavy firepower. Aircraft ML786 is on display at the Imperial War Museum at Duxford. (CLEMENS VASTERS)

SHORT SUNDERLAND MK III

Crew: 9–11

Length: 26.01m (85ft 4in)

Wingspan: 34.4m (112ft 9.5in)

Height: 10.02m (32ft 10.5in)

Gross weight: 26,308kg (58,000lb)

Powerplant: Four × Bristol Pegasus XVIII nine-cylinder, air-cooled radial piston engines

Cruise speed: 286kph (155kts)

Range: 2,860km (1,550nm)

Endurance: 13-14 hours

Armament:

Up to 12 × 0.303in or 0.5in Browning machine guns

Up to 2,000lb of bombs, mines, and depth charges.

LEFT: The Royal Canadian Air Force's 442 Squadron operated the Sunderland from 1942 to 1945. Initially from RAF Castle Archdale in Northern Ireland. (CANADIAN DEPARTMENT OF NATIONAL DEFENCE)

maritime empire and a network of flying boat stations were built around Britain, across the Mediterranean, into the Indian Ocean and the Far East.

Once World War Two started, the Sunderland squadrons found themselves increasingly drawn into the campaign to defeat the U-boats. Britain was ringed with flying boat docks, from Sullom Voe in Shetland, Stranraer and Oban in Scotland, Castle Archdale in Northern Ireland, Pembroke Dock in Wales, and Mount Batten near Plymouth. Many of these sites with their distinctive hangars and launching ramps are still in existence today.

As the war progressed, RAF Coastal Command introduced additional variants with new engines, sensors, and weapons. The Sunderland Mk.3 first appeared in December 1941, and it incorporated many improvements to enhance its sub-hunting capabilities. These included the ASV Mk 2 radar that could detect U-boats on the surface. When the Germans started to fit radar detectors on their submarines, the new improved ASV Mk 3 radar was developed. More fuselage guns were installed, and extra-ammunition was carried.

German U-boat crews feared the Sunderland because of its long endurance - more than 14 hours - and heavy fire power. The aircraft was nicknamed the 'Flying Porcupine' and U-boats tried to avoid getting into gunnery duels with Sunderlands. The flying boats also came out on top in several engagements with German maritime patrol aircraft and bombers trying attack British convoys.

A Sunderland of the Royal Australian Air Force was credited with scoring the type's first unassisted kill of a U-boat in July 1940 in the Western Approaches. By the end of the war, Sunderlands were credited with 26 confirmed U-boat kills and assists in several other kills.

BELOW: A network of bases was established around the North Atlantic to support Sunderland flying boat operations. (IMPERIAL WAR MUSEUM)

Consolidated PBY Catalina

America's Flying Boat

The aircraft that eventually became known as the Consolidated PBY Catalina was the most-built flying boat of World War Two, with 3,281 being constructed in the USA and Canada, along with several hundred in the USSR.

The prototype Consolidated Model 28 first flew in 1935 and it did not appear to have any of the features you would expect on a successful maritime patrol aircraft. Its performance was modest and the PBY, as it was soon dubbed by US Navy crews, was jocularly eventually described as 'the slowest combat aircraft of the war'. But it proved to be a sturdy, reliable aircraft, ideally suited for long patrols over the oceans.

Isaac Laddon designed it, and unusually for the time, it was an all-metal flying boat. The PBY's distinctive high wing configuration was unlike any other flying boat of the time. The US Navy had given the prototype the designation P3Y, but then changed it to PBY because of the aircraft's ability to carry a significant bomb load. PB meant 'patrol bomber', and Y was the manufacturer letter assigned to Consolidated. The first production

model, the PBY-1, was ordered in 1935 and entered service in 1937. It was only after the first hundred had been built that the aircraft's distinctive dorsal observation blisters were added.

The Royal Air Force received its first aircraft in spring of 1941, and it named them the Catalina, after the island in California. Subsequently, the US Navy and other operators adopted the name. Canada called its aircraft the Canso.

The Catalina was designed as a pure flying boat, but in 1939 the first PBY-5A flew. It was an amphibian, with tricycle landing gear. The main wheels retracted upwards in the fuselage sides, under the wing, and remained clearly visible. This meant an increase in weight, and therefore a reduction in range. The RAF preferred the pure flying boat model, and only 11 of the more than 700 Catalinas that it received were amphibious.

CONSOLIDATED PBY CATALINA

Crew: Eight

Length: 19.48m (63ft 11in)

Wingspan: 32m (104ft)

Height: 6.43m (21ft 1in)

Max take-off weight: 16,066kg (35,420lb)

Powerplant: Two × Pratt & Whitney R-1830-92 Twin Wasp piston engines

Cruise speed: 201kph (109kts)

Range: 4,060km (2,190nm)

Armament:

Guns: Three × .30in, two × .50in machine guns blister

Bombs: 4,000lb (of bombs or depth charges)

US Navy instructors flew to Britain to train RAF crews to operate their new Catalinas and in May 1941, a RAF Catalina with an American pilot at the controls took off from Castle Archdale in Northern Ireland. During the mission it found the German battleship *Bismark*, allowing the Royal Navy to find and subsequently sink her.

Catalinas were modified in the course of the war to add improved armament, radar, and search lights, to enhance their submarine hunting capabilities.

RAF, Royal Canadian Air Force and US Navy Catalinas played a prominent part in the Battle of the Atlantic, flying from bases in Britain, Iceland, and Canada. Two RAF Catalina pilots won the Victoria Cross for pressing home attacks against U-boats, this was out of four VC's awarded to Coastal Command personnel in World War Two. Another Canadian Catalina pilot won the VC. In total, Allied Catalinas claimed 40 U-boat kills and shares of several other kills.

ABOVE: The US Navy operated PBY-5A Catalinas during the Battle of the Atlantic from several bases in the North Atlantic theatre. (US NAVY)

BELOW: Canadian Vickers-Limited manufactured the PBV-1A Canso under licence for the Royal Canadian Air Force. One remains airworthy and made an appearance at the 2009 Royal International Air Tattoo at RAF Fairford, Gloucestershire, England. (ADRIAN PINGSTONE)

Consolidated Liberator

The Very Long-Range Aircraft

ABOVE: The first RAF Coastal Command unit to operate the Liberator was 120 Squadron from RAF Aldergrove in Northern Ireland. The squadron went on to be the highest scoring U-boat killing unit of RAF Coastal Command in World War Two. (IMPERIAL WAR MUSEUM)

The mighty Consolidated Liberator was the most important maritime patrol aircraft to join the Battle of the Atlantic. RAF Coastal Command received more than 800 Liberators out of 2,091 delivered to Britain from April 1941.

Although it was originally designed as a heavy bomber for the United States Army Air Forces (USAAF), the aircraft's long range meant its potential for maritime patrol was soon identified. By reducing its bomb-load extra fuel tanks could be fitted to turn it into a very long-range aircraft that could potentially close the air cover 'gap' in the middle of the Atlantic.

After disappointing results in the bombing role, RAF Coastal Command's 120 Squadron received its first Liberators in June 1941 and began flying patrols against U-boats in them three months later. Over the next 18

RIGHT: More than 3,000 of the 18,188 B-24 Liberators built during World War Two were assembled in the Consolidated-Vultee Plant at Fort Worth, Texas for the US military and foreign air arms. (USAF)

months, 120 Squadron was the only RAF unit operating the very long-range aircraft over the Atlantic from bases in Northern Ireland and Iceland. They immediately made a difference, driving U-boats away from vital convoys.

The RAF immediately started to modify its Liberators, fitting ASV Mk II radars, Leigh Light searchlights, underwing rockets and additional machine guns. Its long-range Liberators sacrificed some armour and often gun turrets to save weight, while carrying extra fuel in their bomb-bay tanks. Liberators then had the ability to hunt U-boats by day and by night. The combination of the Leight Light and radar was so effective that many U-boat crews chose to surface during the day so that they could at least see the aircraft attacking them and have a chance to fire their anti-aircraft weaponry in defence.

The Liberator GR Mk V variant proved to be Coastal Command's best shore-based maritime patrol aircraft of World War Two and it eventually prompted the RAF to move away from flying boats for shore-based maritime patrol aircraft. A total of nine Coastal Command squadrons operated the Liberator against the U-boats from 1941 until the end of the war.

The US Army Air Forces (USAAF), US Navy, and RCAF also used the Liberators to hunt U-boats, flying from bases on both sides of the Atlantic and Iceland. Two Royal Canadian Air Force (RCAF) squadrons operated the Liberators from Newfoundland to close 'the gap' from the western side. USAAF Anti-submarine Command Liberators operated from bases in Britain, Morocco, and the eastern seaboard of the United States. In October 1943, these aircraft were transferred to the US Navy.

During the Battle of the Atlantic, 120 Squadron was the highest scoring RAF unit, with 14 confirmed U-boats kills between October 1942 and the end of the war. It is credited with a share in the sinking of three more, plus eight damaged.

RAF Coastal Command Liberators claimed 70 U-boat kills and the RCAF claimed two more. USAAF Liberators participated in sinking 10 U-boats, while US Navy Liberators claimed 13 more kills.

ABOVE: The US Army Air Forces (USAAF) operated the B-24 in bombing roles but the US Navy began to use the very long range version to hunt for submarines in the Battle of the Atlantic. (US ARMY AIR FORCES)

BELOW: The RAF took delivery of its first B-24 in 1941 and used them for maritime patrol, bombing, and transport duties. (CANADIAN DEPARTMENT OF NATIONAL DEFENCE)

CONSOLIDATED LIBERATOR

Crew: 11	
Length: 20.47m (67ft 2in)	
Wingspan: 34m (110ft)	
Height: 5.37m (17ft 7½in)	
Gross weight: 24,948kg (55,000lb)	
Powerplant: Four × Pratt & Whitney R-1830-35 Twin Wasp, R-1830-41, or R-1830-65 14	
Cruise speed: 346kph (187kts)	
Range: 3,888km (2,100nm)	
Armament:	
Guns: 10 × .50in (12.7mm) M2 Browning machine guns in four turrets and two waist positions	
12,800lb of bombs or depth charges	

The Royal Navy Strikes Back

Anti-Submarine Escort and Support Groups

RIGHT: The Flower-class corvette, HMCS *Sackville*, is now moored behind the Maritime Museum of the Atlantic in Halifax, Nova Scotia, and has been restored to her 1944 condition. Canada's navy was second only to the Royal Navy in terms of vessels and personnel committed to the Battle of the Atlantic. (DENNIS JARVIS)

A t the start of the Battle of the Atlantic, the British were critically short of escort vessels. The Royal Navy was thinly spread around the world – fighting the Germans and Italians in the Mediterranean, escorting convoys to Russia and battling the Japanese in the Far East. It crucially lacked escort frigates with the range and endurance to operate effectively in the centre of the North Atlantic. This meant the convoy escorts were so thinly spread that when U-boats attacked, they could not be pursued and sunk. Escorts had to remain with their convoys. So, the Royal Navy was just not able to inflict losses on the U-boats, who could slip away, re-group and attack again with near impunity.

The Admiralty had recognised these weaknesses, even before war began in September 1939 and a crash programme to build long range anti-submarine vessels was launched.

The first ships ordered were the Black Swan-class of escort sloops, which displaced 1,350 tons and were 300ft long. They had a top speed of 20kts so could outrun a U-boat. Up to 1943, 37 were built and they were credited with 29 U-boat kills.

Then came the 925-ton Flower-class of corvette, which were based on commercial whale catchers and so had good sea-worthiness in North Atlantic conditions. In total 294 vessels of the class were built for the British and Canadian navies up to 1943, although many were later

RIGHT: Officers on the bridge of Canadian Flower-class corvette HMCS *Trillium*. (CANADIAN DEPERTMENT OF NATIONAL DEFENCE)

submarines. The performance of ASDIC systems improved during the war, and this made it easier for crews to localise the position of submerged U-boats. Support groups had the job of relentlessly pursuing U-boats, continuously dropping depth charges to keep them underwater until they reached the limit of their air supply and battery power reserves. When these were exhausted, a U-boat would be forced to surface, to either surrender or face destruction.

To allow support groups to pre-empt U-boat attacks by detecting when a wolf pack was approaching a convoy, Royal Navy and Allied escort vessels started to be fitted with radio direction finding equipment, known HF/DF, which could pick up when U-boats were transmitting radio messages. This was an important tactic for the Germans because it allowed a U-boat that spotted a convoy to call other submarines to join the attack. The next upgrade to the escort vessels was the installation of surveillance radars that allowed the detection of U-boats on the surface.

To further enhance the offensive capability of escort vessels, they began to be fitted with forward fire depth charge dispensers to increase the firepower of the escorts. The design of depth charges improved considerably during the war too with fuses being introduced that could be adjusted to detonate at specific depths. This allowed a pattern of explosions to be set to catch U-boats as they dived to escape their pursers.

By 1943, the Royal Navy's flotilla of anti-submarine escort vessels was reaching the peak of its capabilities, both technologically and operationally. The Support Groups became highly trained and drilled, with skilled and aggressive commanders who took the war to the U-boats.

ABOVE: The Flower-class corvette HMS *Jonquil* was one of the workhorses of the Royal Navy's contribution to the Battle of the Atlantic. (IMPERIAL WAR MUSEUM)

LEFT: Captain F J Walker was the most successful U-boat hunter of World War Two. He commanded the Second Escort Group at the height of the Battle of Atlantic. (IMPERIAL WAR MUSEUM)

transferred to other navies. Forty-nine German and four Italian submarines were claimed killed by Flower-class ships.

The ultimate ASW vessel of World War Two were the 1,370-ton River-class frigates. They were designed to be mass produced and as the war progressed, the Loch-class sub-variant with improved features were introduced. The 151 original River-class were built between 1941 and 1944 for use mainly with the British and Canadian navies. The 28 Loch-Class were built from 1944 onwards.

Many of these new ships were operated in so-called Support Groups so they could be detached from convoys to pursue U-boats to destruction. They were progressively equipped with new acoustic sensors, known as ASDIC, which could detect and identify submerged

LEFT: A Hedgehog 24-barrelled anti-submarine mortar mounted on the forecastle of HMS *Westcott*. It was designed to fire forward of warships so U-boats could be engaged as escorts moved against German submarines. (IMPERIAL WAR MUSEUM)

The Decisive Battles

Turning the Tide

The Battle of the Atlantic was the decisive naval engagement of the war against Nazi Germany. Allied naval and air forces defeated the attempt by the Nazi submarine force - the infamous U-boats - to cut off Britain's vital maritime supply lines from North America and the wider British Empire. This battle, or campaign, turned in the first half of 1943 when the Allies brought to bear improved tactics and technology to break the back of the U-boat fleet. With the defeat of the U-boats, the build-up of US troops in Britain ahead of the D-Day landings in northern France in 1944 was able to accelerate. If the U-boats had not been crushed, then there would have been no D-Day.

A few simple data points explain how pivotal the first months of 1943 were. Up to then the Allies were losing more merchant shipping to the U-boats than could be replaced. At the same time, the Germans were able to replace all their U-boat losses with two or three newly built submarines. In 1942, the Allies lost 1,664 merchant ships but German only lost 87 U-boats.

The first months of 1943 would be perilous for Allied convoys crossing the North Atlantic. This peril was magnified by the fact that in the first weeks of 1943, the German B-Dienst code breakers cracked the British

naval codes being used in the North Atlantic and were soon reading all the radio traffic to two large convoys, codenamed SC-122 and HX-229, which were heading to Britain from Canada and United States.

Dönitz began mobilising his U-boat wolf packs to intercept the convoys that contained 98 merchant vessels, some of which could not make more than 10kts in the heavy Atlantic storms and were protected by a total of 13 escort vessels. The U-boat commanders expected easy pickings.

First Dönitz had to confirm the exact position of the convoys and then mass his U-boats from three wolf packs, each containing more than a dozen submarines, to strike at them as they moved east from March 6. He ordered the nearest U-boats to move to intercept and then radio contact information so that the wolf packs could strike. The winter weather initially helped protect the convoys, but the elite U-boat commanders knew their trade and soon had targets in their sights.

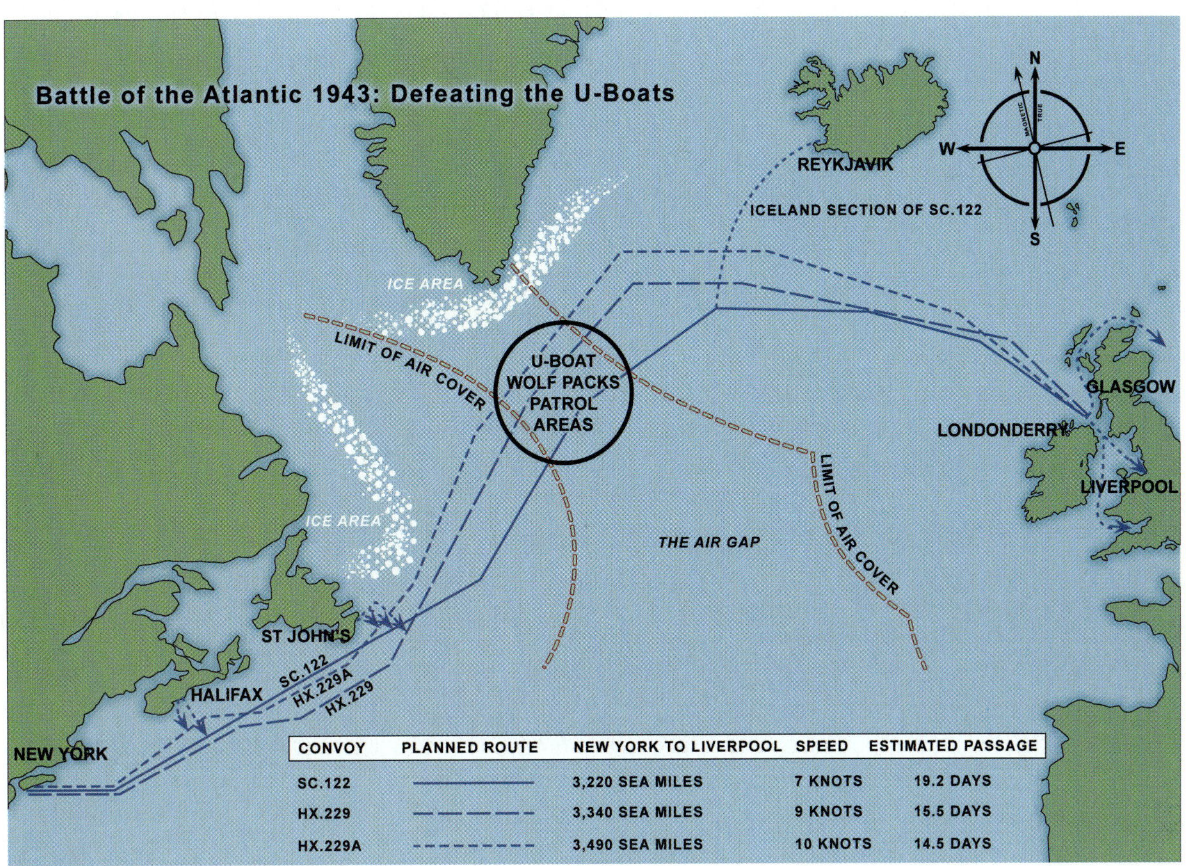

CONVOY	PLANNED ROUTE	NEW YORK TO LIVERPOOL	SPEED	ESTIMATED PASSAGE
SC.122	——————	3,220 SEA MILES	7 KNOTS	19.2 DAYS
HX.229	– – – – –	3,340 SEA MILES	9 KNOTS	15.5 DAYS
HX.229A	- - - - -	3,490 SEA MILES	10 KNOTS	14.5 DAYS

LEFT: Allied convoys were highly vulnerable in the centre of the North Atlantic where U-boats could operate on the surface with impunity until 'the gap' was closed. (KEY PUBLISHING)

One U-boat by accident stumbled on SC-122 in the storms and quickly reported its position. In the gloom of the early hours of March 16, the U-boats struck and by dawn eight ships had been sunk or abandoned by their crews. The following night another wolf pack attacked HX-229 and sank another four merchant vessels. Another vessel fell prey to a daylight attack during March 17.

Fortunately, SC-122 had now crossed 'the gap' and maritime patrol aircraft from Iceland arrived overhead to escort it for the remainder of its journey. The pursuing U-boats fell back and concentrated their attention on HX-229. Eleven U-boats had been massed for the attack and struck during the daytime on March 17. The bad weather meant the U-boats could attack on the surface, with little chance of being spotted. During the course of eight hours, 10 ships were hit, setting them on fire and forcing their crews to abandon ship. The hard-pressed escort vessels struggled to pick-up the traumatised survivors from the freezing sea. There were no warships available to counterattack against the U-boats. It was only when the first Allied aircraft arrived overhead in the late afternoon that the first U-boat was forced to dive to avoid attack. The wolf pack broke off its attack to re-group, re-fuel, and re-arm.

Another wolf pack had caught up with SC-122 and positioned itself to attack at night, when the Allied aircraft could not protect it. During the night of March 17, the U-boats managed to pick off two more merchant ships.

Despite the presence of air cover on March 17, the U-boats tried to press home their attacks on the convoys, but the escorts were now able to take the fight to the enemy, forcing several U-boats to break off their surface attacks and dive. One U-boat captain launched an underwater attack on HX-229 and managed to penetrate the escort screen to sink two merchant vessels.

This cat and mouse game continued for two more days as the wolf packs harried the convoys and attempted to dodge past the escort screen and Allied air patrols. Two more ships were picked off before the U-boats lost contact with the convoys. A week later the survivors of the two convoys arrived in British ports. It had been a brutal battle in which 22 merchant ships had been sunk and 300 seamen died. »

BELOW: Britain was dependent on US Navy tankers, such as *Hat Creek*, to keep its planes, tanks and ships fighting. (US NAVY)

The attacking wolf packs had mustered 38 U-boats to engage SC-122 and HX-229 and inflicted carnage for minimal losses. Only one U-boat was sunk during the course of the running battle, when U-384 was found on the surface and sunk by a RAF B-17 Flying Fortress. Eight U-boats were engaged by escorts and RAF aircraft, suffering varying degrees of damage but they were all able to return to base for repair.

From the Allies perspective, this was the low point of the Battle of the Atlantic, with a senior Royal Navy commander commenting: "It appeared possible that we should not be able to regard convoy as an effective system of defence."

Nine more merchant ships were lost in convoys during April but in May the tide turned against the U-boats. Convoy ONS 5 comprising 42 merchant ships and seven escorts sailed from Liverpool on April 21 and headed for North America to pick up war cargo. By early May, it had reached the centre of the Atlantic and Dönitz ordered 43 U-boats to mass against it. At first the U-boats attacked with impunity. Two merchant ships were sunk on May 4 and the following day 10 more went to the bottom.

The Admiralty now sent reinforcements to bolster the protection of ONS 5 and for the first time committed support groups to convoy battle in the North Atlantic. After a rapid passage from Newfoundland the 3rd Support Group, with four destroyers, joined the convoy on May 3 and two days later, they were joined by the 1st Support Group with five frigates. RCAF Catalina flying boats were now within range of the convoy and could aid the fight back.

These reinforcements soon turned the tables on the U-boats. Using their radio direction finding equipment, the support groups were able to mass ships to intercept U-boats as they approached the convoy, forcing them to submerge and then lay down barrages of depth charges. The British frigates were then able to stay on station to hunt down the U-boats, tracking them with sonar and dropping more depth charges. These duels lasted several hours at a time and while the frigates attacked, the rest of the convoy was able to continue on its way.

On May 5, two U-boats were depth charged and destroyed. Four more were sunk the following day, including one which was rammed by a Royal Navy frigate. In the course

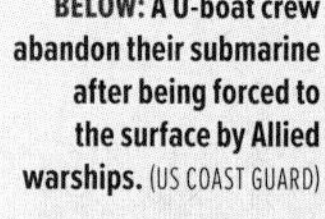

of this battle, two more U-boats were spotted by British and Canadian patrol aircraft and sunk. A further seven U-boats were damaged in engagements with the frigates and patrol aircraft.

Subsequent attacks on convoys saw similar losses for the U-boats, for negligible losses in merchant shipping, with five U-boats being lost for the same number of merchant vessels. Then the next convoy made it across the Atlantic without losing any ships and the escorts, support groups and patrol aircraft sank five U-boats. This set the trend for the rest of the war.

On May 6, 1943, Dönitz radioed his U-boat captains to order them to call off the attacks on ONS-5, citing heavy losses and strong escort coverage. Soon the U-boat crews nicknamed May 1943 as 'Black May' after 40 U-boats failed to return from war cruises in the Atlantic. On board one of those U-boats, U-954, was Doenitz's own son Peter who was lost along with the rest of the crew. By the May 23, almost a third of Germany's Atlantic U-boat fleet had been lost.

Remarkably, the code breakers in Bletchley Park were able to decode orders from Dönitz on May 24, calling an end to the wolf pack campaign in the North Atlantic. The Admiralty was able to read their foe's message long before many of his U-boats were able to decode the signals themselves.

Dönitz acknowledged that the Allied advances in anti-submarine war had nullified the wolf pack tactics and rendered the majority of his fleet obsolete. He withdrew his fleet from the North Atlantic convoy routes but promised they would be back when faster, better equipped U-boats were available. They never materialised. The following month 17 U-boats were sunk and 37 were lost in July 1943, setting the irreversible decline of the U-boat fleet. In 1943, the Germans

ABOVE: Synthetic Aperture Sonar (SAS) showing the remains of U-*853*. She was a type IXC/40 German submarine launched on March 11, 1943, and patrolled off the US Atlantic coast during World War II. (US OFFICE OF OCEAN EXPLORATION AND RESEARCH/KRAKEN ROBOTICS)

LEFT: RAF Coastal Command gunners strafe a U-boat that was caught on the surface by a Sunderland flying boat. Survivors of the crew can be seen in the water at the bottom right of the photo. (CANADIAN DEPARTMENT OF NATIONAL DEFENCE)

lost a total of 258 U-boats, of which 90 were confirmed sunk by aircraft and a further 51 were damaged in air attacks.

In his memoirs, written 15 years later, Dönitz admitted that 'Black May' marked the German defeat in the Battle of the Atlantic. While the war continued for another two years and both merchant and U-boat crews suffered losses, the U-boat was never again to enjoy the success it had achieved during the time of the wolf packs.

Allied shipping losses were starting to drop dramatically as well and, by the end of 1943 it was routine for convoys to cross the Atlantic without losses. D-Day was safe and went ahead as scheduled in June 1944.

LEFT: The US Coast Guard cutter *Spencer* found and depth charged U-*175*, 500nm southwest of Ireland on April 17, 1943, forcing the U-boat to the surface, where the crew surrendered before it sank. (US NATIONAL ARCHIVES)

Soviet Submarine Threat

Red Storm Rising

In July 1951, when the US Congress authorised the construction of the world's first nuclear power submarine, the USS *Nautilus*, it was no surprise that their Cold War adversary, the Soviet Union, would soon follow suit. This was the era of the nuclear arms race, so once one side made a move, it was quickly countered by the other.

Nuclear power offered the potential to transform submarine war. The German U-boats had given the British a run for their money in the Battle of the Atlantic, but the Royal Navy and Royal Air Force soon realised the weaknesses in the Nazi underwater craft. They had to surface to recharge their batteries or communicate and became vulnerable to attack, largely from the air. Even the invention of the

snorkel that allowed submarines to run their diesel engines underwater, still required part of the vessel to break the surface and could be detected by radar or observed by spotters.

The advent of nuclear power meant submarines never had to surface and expose themselves, risking detection. This heralded the era of true submarines. When combined with other technologies to provide crew with unlimited fresh air and drinking water it meant the only effective limit of the time a nuclear-power submarine could remain underwater was the amount of food it could carry to keep the crew fed. Key technologies became oxygen generators that recycled fresh air and while diesel engines required air for combustion, nuclear powerplants did not. Drinking water can also be created for the crew from sea water, by a process known as reverse osmosis.

Just like the Americans, the Soviet navy recognised how nuclear-power submarines could transform naval warfare. The then leader of the Soviet Union, Josef Stalin, never had much interest in naval strategy but he recognised that nuclear weapons and nuclear power offered the potential to up end the old global power structures. The atomic bomb attacks on Japan in 1945 that ended World War Two showed that only countries with nuclear weapons would dictate world affairs. Stalin wanted to make sure he did not have to bend to the will of the world's only nuclear power, the United States of America. So when, in 1952, his admirals proposed building a nuclear-powered submarine to counter the building of the USS *Nautilus,* Stalin immediately gave the go ahead.

The result was the Project 627 submarine, or as it was known in the West, the November-class. This was a project of huge importance to the Soviets and eventually 135 organisations - 20 design bureaus, 35 research institutes, and 80 industrial works – became involved. In August 1957, the first of class, the *K-3,* was launched at the SEVMASH shipyard in the northern port city of Molotovsk, which is now known as Severodvinsk, and set sail the following July. This shipyard became the home of Soviet submarine building and is now Russia's sole »

ABOVE: In the 1980s, US intelligence envisaged that the Soviets would protect their nuclear submarine fleet in tunnels for protection against US nuclear strikes. This proved fanciful. (US DOD/DIA)

BELOW: Soviet submarine building shipyards were hidden from view of foreign observers during the Cold War, but details have since emerged from behind the Iron Curtain. (@SATURNAX1)

nuclear-powered submarine building yard. It is Russia's equivalent of Barrow-in-Furness in Britain or Groton in Connecticut.

By this time Stalin was dead and the Soviet navy had a new chief, Admiral Sergey Gorshkov, who had ambitions to challenge the US Navy for dominance of the high seas. A hero for his role as commander of Soviet naval units in the Black Sea during World War Two, Gorshkov was a highly practical officer who became expert at bringing new vessels and weapons into service. His famous motto was "'Better' is the enemy of 'Good Enough'".

Stalin's successor as the Soviet Union's premier, Nikita Khrushchev saw naval expansion as a key strategy to overtake America in the nuclear arms race and he first made Gorshkov commander-in-chief of the Soviet Navy in January 1956, and then six years later promoted him to deputy defence minister. Gorshkov's plan was to achieve naval parity with the West by the 1970s. This included the widespread adoption of nuclear weapons across the Soviet fleet, through the building of a large flotilla of ballistic missile firing submarines and attack boats. In order to project

Soviet military power, Gorshkov sent his ships and submarines on lengthy cruises and formed operational squadrons in the Mediterranean Sea as well as the Atlantic, Pacific, and Indian Oceans. He was soon dubbed the 'father of the Soviet blue-water navy'.

Gorshkov quickly recognised that the original idea behind the K-3 – to launch nuclear-tipped torpedoes to devastate American ports – was fanciful and he directed that the submarine be optimised to take on US Navy warships and submarines with conventional torpedoes. She was the first Soviet hunter-killer submarine, or SSN.

The K-3 was a record breaker. In June 1962, she was the first Soviet submarine to sail under the North Pole and surface through the ice cap. For this voyage, she was named *Leninsky Komsomol*, after the Soviet youth organisation. This was a rare honour, as Soviet submarines were usually only granted an alpha-numeric designation rather than names. Her crew, rather than training in military operations, began taking part in publicity events to promote the Soviet navy's achievements. This was an honour only granted to Soviet

astronauts of this era, such as the first man in space, Yuri Gagarin.

The submarine remained in service as an experimental vessel until she was decommissioned in 1988. Her important role in Soviet and Russian naval history led to her being preserved at the Museum of Naval Glory on Kronstadt Island, close to St Petersburg. One of the first visitors to see her when the museum opened in the summer of 2023 was Russian President Vladimir Putin, whose father served in the Soviet submarine fleet in the 1930s.

Even before the K-3 had sailed on her maiden voyage, the Soviet navy was pushing forward with designs for new, bigger, and more powerful nuclear-powered submarines. Work began in 1956 on the Project 658 nuclear-powered, ballistic missile firing submarine, or SSBN. This was dubbed the Hotel-class by the West, and she was the first Soviet submarine that could fire strategic nuclear weapons while submerged. By the standards of today, its firepower was modest. It housed three R-13 missiles, which had a range of 600km, in her sail. But for the first time the Soviet Navy could strike at America's cities from the sea. Eventually eight entered service between 1960 and 1962.

During the 1960s, new Soviet nuclear submarines came on line at a break neck speed as Soviet designers and engineers overcame many of the problems that plagued the early boats. Nuclear submarines started to be built at yards across the Soviet Union, including in Leningrad, Nizhny Novgorod, and Komsomolsk-on-Amur in the Soviet Far East.

Victor and Yankee Class

The Project 627 boats eventually gave way to the improved Project 671, or Victor-class, attack submarines. Improved Project 667, or Yankee-class, SSBNs replaced the old Hotel-class boats from 1964, which featured a missile compartment behind the sail. This became the distinctive feature of Soviet and then Russian SSBNs. The Yankee-class boats and their successors effectively neutralised

the ability of the US to launch a first strike against land-based Soviet nuclear forces and brought stability to the arms race. They guaranteed mutually assured destruction (MAD) and allowed the first arms control moves to be made in the late 1960s and 1970s to limit strategic nuclear arsenals.

The Soviet Navy also fielded a unique type of submarine, the guided missile boat, or SSGN, which were armed with both nuclear and conventional armed cruise missiles. These were intended to strike at US Navy carrier battle groups or naval bases. Their missiles were usually fitted in a launcher, mounted in the forward hull.

Through the 1950s and 1960s, the Soviets poured huge resources into developing their nuclear-powered submarines but at the same time continued building conventionally powered submarines. They captured some of the German U-boats which

featured advanced snorkel and battery technology, as well as many Nazi submarine designers, who were immediately put to work building submarines for their new masters. Many of the weapon and sensor technologies destined for nuclear boats, were tried out in conventional submarines first.

Soviet first and second-generation nuclear-powered submarines were not as advanced as their US and British counterparts. They were smaller, less reliable and, crucially, nosier. This was critical disadvantage that Western anti-submarine forces tried to exploit. Alerted to some of their weaknesses by spies in the US Navy and Royal Navy, the Soviets moved quickly to field super-quiet and super-fast submarines.

The ultimate Soviet attack submarine was the Project 705, or Alpha-class, which had the distinction of being the fastest »

BELOW: The Hotel-class were the first nuclear-powered submarines fitted with Soviet ballistic missiles. (US DOD)

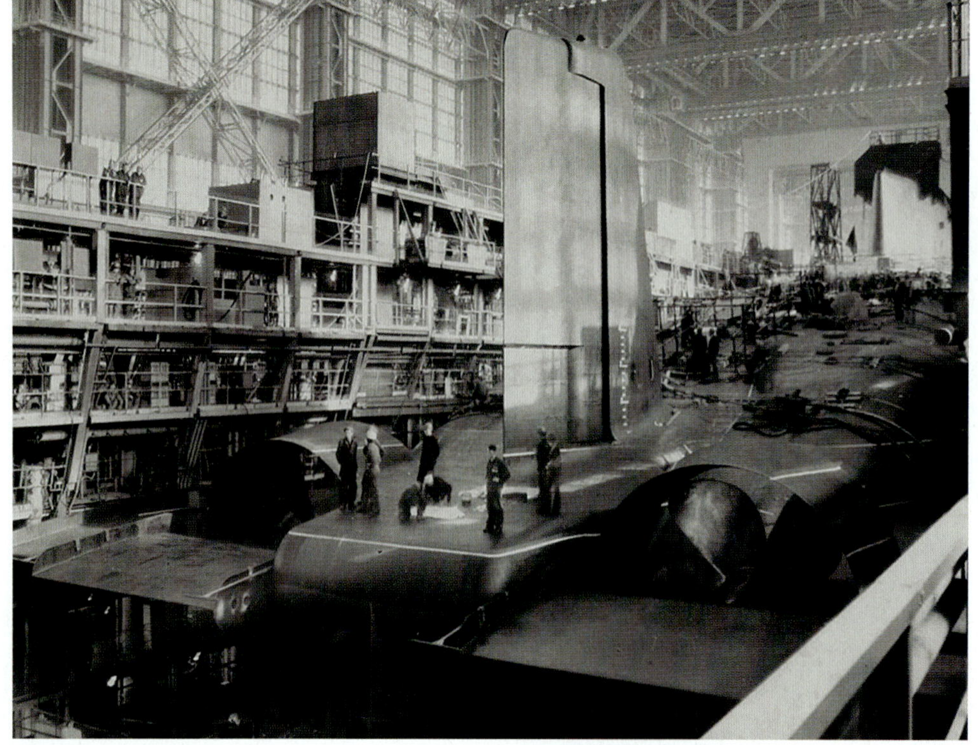

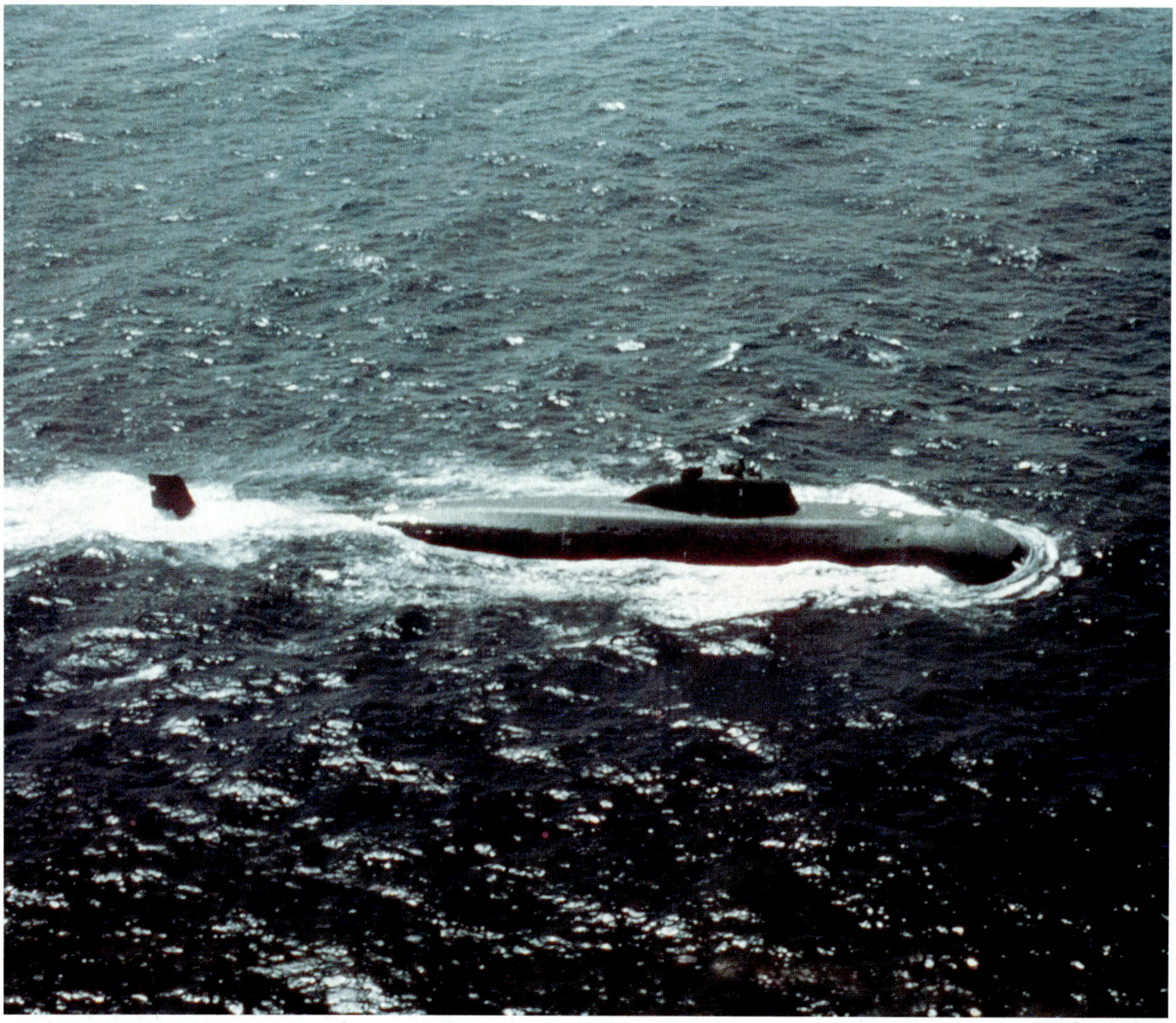

RIGHT: From 1967, 48 Victor-class nuclear-powered attack submarines entered Soviet Navy service and they remained the work horse of Moscow's fleet until the end of the Cold War. (US DOD)

BELOW: A Typhoon-class SSBN under construction at the SEVMASH shipyard at Severodvinsk in the Arkhangelsk in the 1980s. This yard has been at the centre of Soviet and Russian submarine development since the 1950s. (@SATURNAX1)

submarine ever built, with a remarkable submerged top speed of 41kts. No Western submarine or torpedo could catch the Alpha, which could also accelerate and manoeuvre with an agility that was unmatched. They were built from titanium, which reduced weight, confused magnetic anomaly detection (MAD) devices, and allowed them to dive deeper - 2,200ft - than any western submarine. The boat was highly automated, with only 31 crew. This allowed more room for machinery and weapons.

Work on the Alpha-class got underway in 1964 and the first boat went to sea in 1971. When US and British submarines started to track them and their performance, it caused panic in Western capitals. Crash programmes were launched to build better torpedoes and submarines to match them.

Fortunately for Western navies, the Alphas had major short comings that meant that only eight were ever built and the ones that did join the Soviet fleet only rarely put to sea. Building the submarine's titanium hull was far more expensive and more time consuming than other boats. Its innovative lead-cooled fast reactor design allowed a tremendous amount of power to be generated in a compact space, hence the boat's impressive speed and acceleration. However, it also created staggering maintenance problems, few of which could be resolved by the small crew when the boat was submerged. Soviet-era dockyard workers also lacked the skills to keep the boats in working order.

The Alpha-class was ahead of its time. It showed the ambition of the Soviet navy, but the technology

was just too advanced to be made reliable. In the 1980s, a successor, the Project 945, or Sierra-class, started to enter service. This featured the titanium hull and many other features taken from the Alpha-class, but it made them work on a sustained basis. They were still significantly more expensive than any previous submarine and only three had entered service by the time the Soviet Union dissolved at the end of 1991.

The Soviet submarine force was at its zenith in the early 1980s. The 1983 edition of *Jane's Fighting Ships* records it as having 69 SSBNs, 48 SGNs and 62 SSNs, as well as 180 conventionally powered boats. This compared to the US Navy's 40 SSBNs and 88 SSNs. Gorshkov had achieved his ambition of turning the Soviet submarine fleet into a force to be reckoned with.

ABOVE: Alpha-class nuclear-powered attack boats revolutionised the Soviet submarine fleet in the 1970s and 1980s because of their high speed and ultra-quiet characteristics. (TASS)

LEFT: When the Soviet submarine, *B-59*, was forced to the surface near Cuba in October 1962 by the US Navy it convinced the Soviet Navy high command that nuclear submarines were the future. (US NAVY)

Cold War Confrontation

East verse West

RIGHT: A US Navy Lockheed SP-2H Neptune of patrol squadron VP-18 overflies a Soviet freighter carrying 12 Il-28 airplanes back to the Soviet Union from Cuba in December 1962. (US NAVY)

BELOW: Sikorsky's SH-3 Sea King became the default NATO standard anti-submarine helicopter in the 1970s and 1980s, thanks to its impressive performance and effective sensors. This is a Canadian CH-124 Sea King, which were licence produced in Quebec by United Aircraft of Canada. (US NAVY)

At the height of what became known as the Cold War, the West's anti-submarine forces found themselves engaged in a new struggle, against a new foe. Although a shot was never fired against the Soviet Navy during the Cold War, the 40 year-long East-West confrontation that ended in 1989 with the collapse of the Berlin Wall saw dramatic advances in anti-submarine technology and tactics.

The ships and planes that had won the Battle of Atlantic were redundant in the age of nuclear-powered submarines that could remain underwater for months at a time. New approaches were needed for a new era.

The US and its NATO allies were not at war with the Soviet Union but the two power blocs feared war

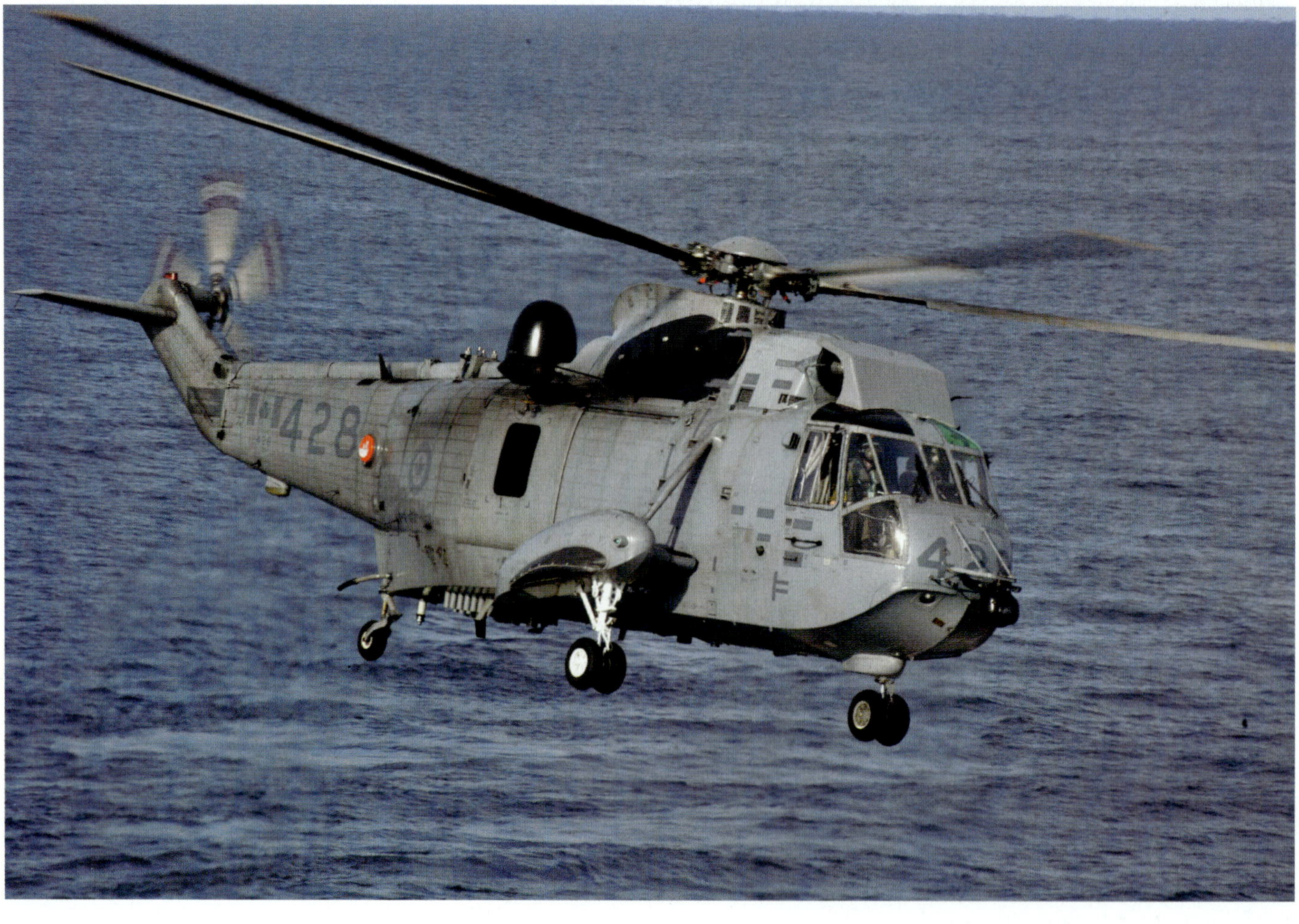

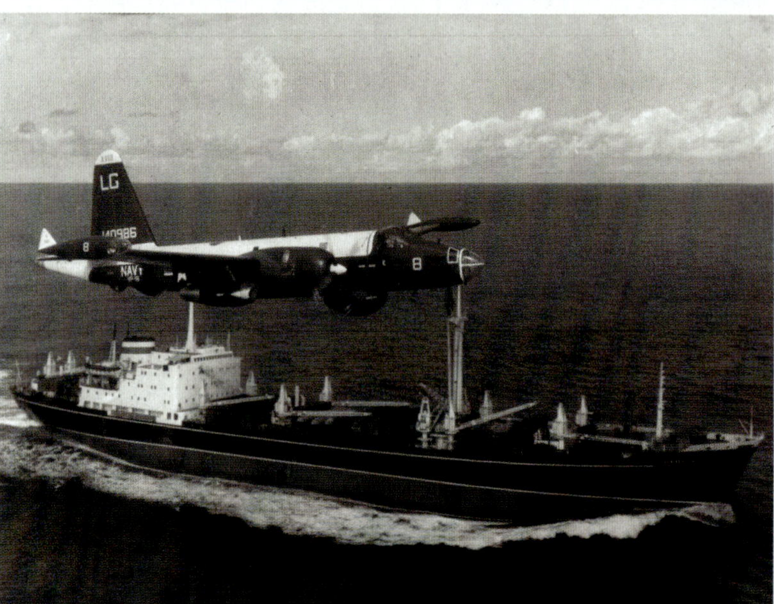

could break out at any time. Both sides built up their conventional and nuclear forces to deter war. By making conflict unimaginably destructive, no one would try to cross the Iron Curtain that divided East and West. Nuclear Armageddon would produce no winners, so said the logic of mutual assured destruction, or MAD.

If war should break out, both sides envisaged only employing conventional weapons at first to avoid escalation to the use of strategic nuclear weapons. Naval forces played an important part in both sides war planning because a large part of their nuclear arsenals was installed in nuclear-powered submarines.

For Western naval chiefs, led by the US Navy and British Royal Navy, this meant their anti-submarine strategy had to very different from that adopted during World War Two.

The founding of the NATO alliance in 1949 opened the way for the establishment of allied naval headquarters covering European and North Atlantic waters. Allied naval and maritime patrol aircraft operations could be co-ordinated, just as in World War Two. Joint training exercises built up skills and expertise, while allied research centres developed the latest underwater surveillance technology and weapons. Western defence companies were able to reduce costs by selling their anti-submarine products across NATO armed forces. NATO naval commanders also developed joint war plans to enable alliance forces to be ready for action should the Cold War turn hot.

Finding Soviet nuclear-powered submarines armed with intercontinental ballistic missiles that could devastate NATO cities was a top priority. Unlike in the U-boat fleet, the Soviet navy did not rely on a centralised radio system to control its operations. A new Ultra would not provide the allies with the inside track on Soviet submarine movements.

Allied intelligence turned to other technology. Soviet naval bases were put under 24/7 satellite surveillance so as soon as a submarine slipped its moorings a massive monitoring apparatus could spring into action. Out in the Pacific and Atlantic oceans, the US Navy established the Sound Surveillance System (SOSUS) network of underwater sonar arrays. These were fixed on the ocean floor and were linked to monitoring stations by giant cables. They were so sensitive they could even identify specific Soviet submarines from their unique acoustic signatures.

When Soviet submarines left port, they passed over SOSUS lines allowing NATO naval commanders to track them as they headed out into open sea. This is when NATO maritime patrol aircraft and submarines took over.

The best weapon to kill - or at least track - a nuclear submarine is another nuclear submarine. So, the US and British navies began forward deploying their attack submarines in 'patrol boxes' just outside Soviet naval bases. If a Soviet submarine headed out in the Atlantic, a US or British attack boat would trail them, trying to maintain enough distance to remain undetected.

Out in the North Atlantic, US Navy, Dutch, Norwegian, British, French, German and Canadian aircraft would be scrambled to take over trailing the Soviet submarines. These aircraft >>

ABOVE: Catching a Soviet submarine on the surface was ambition of every NATO maritime patrol aircraft crew. It demonstrated their prowess and also allowed the collection of important technical intelligence, about the status of Soviet submarines. (US NAVY)

BELOW: A US Navy Lockheed P-3C Orion aircraft of patrol squadron VP-56 taxies along the flight line at Naval Air Station Keflavik, Iceland, in 1977. The Icelandic base was a key hub for NATO maritime patrol aircraft operating in the North Atlantic region. (US NAVY)

were equipped with hundreds of sonobuoys, which were mini sonar devices that were dropped in the sea and transmitted tracking information back to operators in the patrol aircraft. This allowed them to locate and track submerged submarines. Over the decades, the capability of sonobuoys improved dramatically, allowing submarines to be detected at long ranges and for sustained periods. The computing power of the terminals on patrol aircraft also improved progressively so multiple sonobuoys could be controlled by operators. New battery technology also allowed sonobuoy fields to remain active for longer. Better data transmitters meant the controlling patrol aircraft could set up larger sonobuoy fields.

This became the great duel as the rival forces jockeyed for advantage. Rival submarine commanders would try get as close as possible to each other, to demonstrate the superiority of the technology and skill. Likewise, the maritime patrol aircraft crews would try to intimidate Soviet submarine crews by sowing sonobuoy fields across the path. Real weapons were not released. Advantage was gained by the collection of vital intelligence, such as acoustic signatures of submarines, or by forcing an opponent to reveal new features of their submarines.

If an East-West war had broken out, NATO naval commanders hoped that by having as detailed as possible plots of the position of every Soviet submarine at sea, they would be able deliver a rapid knockout blow against them. This would cripple the number of ballistic missiles the Soviet navy could contribute to a nuclear exchange. Hitting the Soviet attack submarine fleet would also reduce its ability to sink supply ships heading to Europe from the New

World. It is a moot point whether NATO's anti-submarine forces could achieve a clean sweep against every Soviet submarine at sea, but they wanted to give it a good go.

Nuclear-powered attack submarines would have a key role in dispatching any Soviet boats they were trailing but by the 1970s the Soviet had devised a new strategy to try to protect their missile firing submarines. It created the so-called 'bastion' concept, where it formed a defensive ring of attack submarines, anti-submarine warships and its own maritime patrol aircraft around the Barents Sea, close to the Soviet Northern Fleet's home bases on the Kola Peninsula.

Western hunter-killer submarines would have to fight their way through this ring of steel to reach the Soviet missile firing boats. The 1960s and 1970s saw dramatic improvements in the anti-submarine capabilities of helicopters embarked on warships. This improvement was intended to

NATO AND ALLIED MARITIME PATROL UNITS, 1980		
Unit	**Aircraft**	**Home Base**
NATO		
German Naval Aviation		
Naval Air Wing 3 (MFG 3) "Graf Zeppelin"	Atlantic	Nordholz Naval Airbase
Royal Canadian Air Force		
404 Long Range Patrol and Training Squadron	CP-107	CFB Greenwood
405 Long Range Patrol Squadron	CP-107	CFB Greenwood
415 Long Range Patrol Force Development Squadron	CP-107	CFB Sommerville
407 Long Range Patrol Squadron	CP-107	CFB Comox
French Naval Aviation		
21 Flottille	Atlantic	Nimes-Garons
22 Flottille	Atlantic	Nimes-Garons
23 Flottille	Atlantic	Lann-Bihoue
24 Flottille	Atlantic	Lann-Bihoue
25 Flottille	SP-2H	Lann-Bihoue
Italian Navy		
87 Gruppo	Atlantic	Sigonella
88 Gruppo	Atlantic	Cagliari-Elmas
Royal Netherlands Air Force		
320 Squadron	P2V-7	Valkenburg
321 Squadron	Atlantic	Valkenburg
Royal Norwegian Air Force		
333 Squadron	P-3B	Andoya Air Station
Portuguese Air Force		
62 Operational Group	P2V-5	Montijo
Royal Air Force		
42 (Torpedo Bomber) Squadron	Nimrod MR1	RAF St Mawagan
120 Squadron	Nimrod MR1/2	RAF Kinloss
201 Squadron	Nimrod MR1/2	RAF Kinloss
206 Squadron	Nimrod MR1/2	RAF Kinloss
236 Operational Conversion Unit	Nimrod MR1/2	RAF St Mawagan
Allied		
Royal Australian Air Force		
10 Squadron	P-3C	RAAF Townsville
11 Squadron	P-3B	RAAF Base Edinburgh
Japanese Maritime Self Defense Force		
1 Squadron	P-2J	Kanoya
11 Squadron	S-2	Kanoya
2 Squadron	P-2J	Hachinoe
4 Squadron	P-2J/H	Hachinoe
3 Squadron	P-2J	Atsugi
14 Squadron	S-3	Atsugi
31 Squadron	PS-1/Us-!	Iwakumi
Royal New Zealand Air Force		
5 Squadron	P-3B	RNZAF Base Wenaupai
Spainish Air Force (joined NATO 1982)		
221 Squadron	P-3B	La Parma

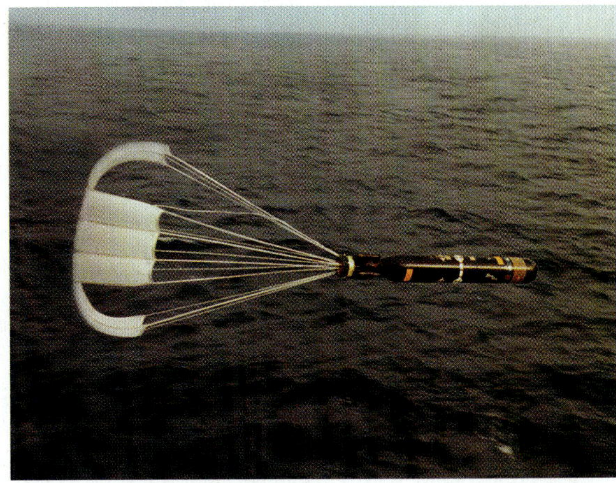

ABOVE: The Stingray light homing torpedo was developed by GEC-Marconi in the late 1970s and early 1980s for use by Royal Navy warships and helicopters, as well as RAF Nimrods. (BAE SYSTEMS)

allow NATO naval tasks groups to attack the Soviet SSBN bastion.

The early versions of the iconic Sikorsky S-3 Sea King helicopter could both drop sonobuoys, and it had a newly developed dipping sonar. This was a winch mounted system that lowered the sonar array into the water. Patrol aircraft and helicopters flying from anti-submarine frigates would often be teamed up to keep Soviet submarines under surveillance so the warships could take over the hunt when patrol aircraft had to return to base to refuel.

A generation of NATO anti-submarine warriors lived and breathed this great duel with their Soviet opponents. No shots or torpedoes were ever fired in anger but hundreds of aircrew and submariners lost their lives in accidents above or underneath the icy North Atlantic. The underwater dimension of the Cold War was never front-page news, but it was a vital element in convincing the leaders of the rival blocs that a surprise attack should not be risked.

BELOW: A Nimrod MR2 mission controller during a North Atlantic patrol. (TIM RIPLEY)

SOSUS

Directing the West's Anti-Submarine Campaign

ABOVE: The SOSUS network was established and maintained by a fleet of cable repair ship, such as the USS *Neptune*.
(US NAVY)

RIGHT: The US Naval Facility at Nantucket, Massachusetts, was control centre of a SOSUS array during the Cold War.
(US NAVY)

In 1949, US scientists were tasked to develop a network of underwater listening stations that could detect Soviet submarines across the length and breadth of the Atlantic and Pacific Oceans.

The scope and ambition of the project were never revealed in public until 1991 when the great Cold War underwater duel had been relegated to history.

The system was soon known to the US Navy and selected allied personnel as Sound Surveillance System, or SOSUS. It was so secret that the whole effort was given the cover name Project Caesar and participating personnel were instructed to tell relatives and friends they were working on a civilian oceanographic research project. Their cover story was that they were studying undersea volcanic eruptions and whales, not tracking Soviet submarines.

A network of highly sensitive, low frequency hydrophones was laid in the North Atlantic and Northern Pacific oceans, connected to shore stations by long undersea cables. When Soviet submarines were detected, the bearing and range were reported to a central command hub,

LEFT: In 1985, dubbed by the press as the 'Year of the Spy', former US Navy warrant officer John Anthony Walker, Jr. was arrested for selling the secrets of the SOSUS network to the Soviet Union. He had been active as a Communist agent since 1967. (US FEDERAL BUREAU OF INVESTIGATION)

where the details were triangulated to create a near exact location. The acoustic signatures were also recorded and eventually every Soviet, US and allied submarine could be identified by the tell-tale noises generated by their propellers and machinery.

The first experimental array and control station was built in the Bahamas in 1951 and over the next three decades dozens more arrays were added, as well as mobile arrays towed by large ships. An indication of the power of the system was the first detection, recognition and reporting on July 6, 1962, of a Soviet nuclear submarine coming into the Atlantic through the Greenland-Iceland-United Kingdom (GIUK) gap by an array terminating in Barbados.

As the Cold War escalated, the importance of SOSUS grew. Finding a submerged nuclear submarine in the depths of the North Atlantic was akin to finding a proverbial needle in a hay stack. SOSUS allowed individual ships, submarines, or maritime patrol aircraft to be dispatched to specific areas of sea to begin trying to find a Soviet submarine. One veteran Royal Navy officer serving during the 1970s and 1980s later said it was almost never the case that NATO anti-submarine forces found a Soviet submarine without being first cued by SOSUS.

So sensitive was the existence of SOSUS that even within the US Navy and NATO no reference was made directly to SOSUS intelligence. Reports from SOSUS arrived in the specially formatted messages, code named RAINFORM, to disguise their source.

The security blanket wrapped around SOSUS was broken in the late 1960s when US Navy Chief Warrant Officer John Walker turned over a cache of naval secrets to the Soviets, including documents detailing the existence and performance of the SOSUS network. This breach reportedly alerted the Soviet navy to how noisy their submarines were and led to the installation of sound reduction features on many of them.

The most importance success of the SOSUS system was the detection of lost submarines, including the USS *Thresher* in 1963 and USS *Scorpion* in 1968. An explosion on a Soviet ballistic missile submarine in 1968 was detected and this allowed the US Central Intelligence Agency, with the help of reclusive inventor Howard Hughes, to launch an effort to recover the sunken vessel.

SOSUS was the Cold War equivalent of the Ultra code-breaking organisation, and it gave US and NATO submarine hunters a critical advantage in the great duel with the Soviets.

BELOW: The SOSUS network detected an explosion in 1968 that sank a Soviet submarine. The US Central Intelligence Agency teamed up with the reclusive tycoon Howard Hughes to bring the submarine to the surface using a purpose-built ship, the ***Glomar Explorer***. (US GOVERNMENT)

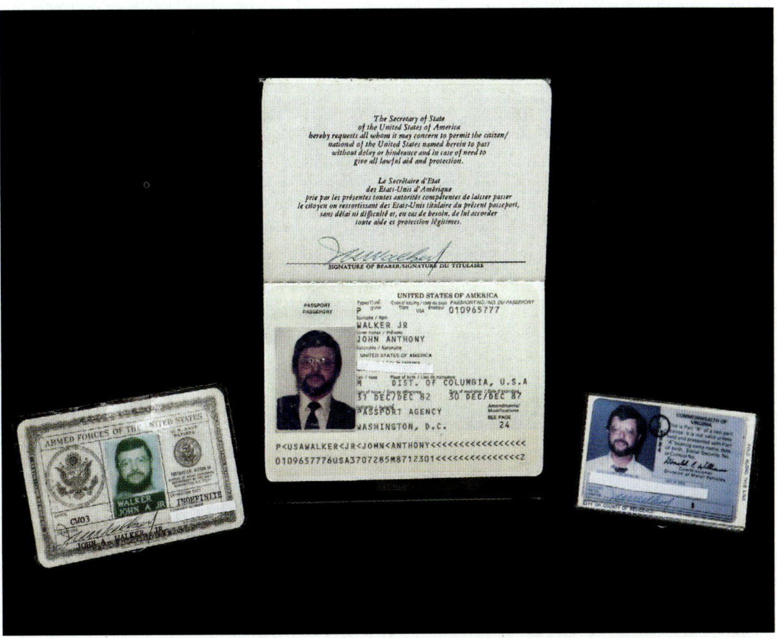

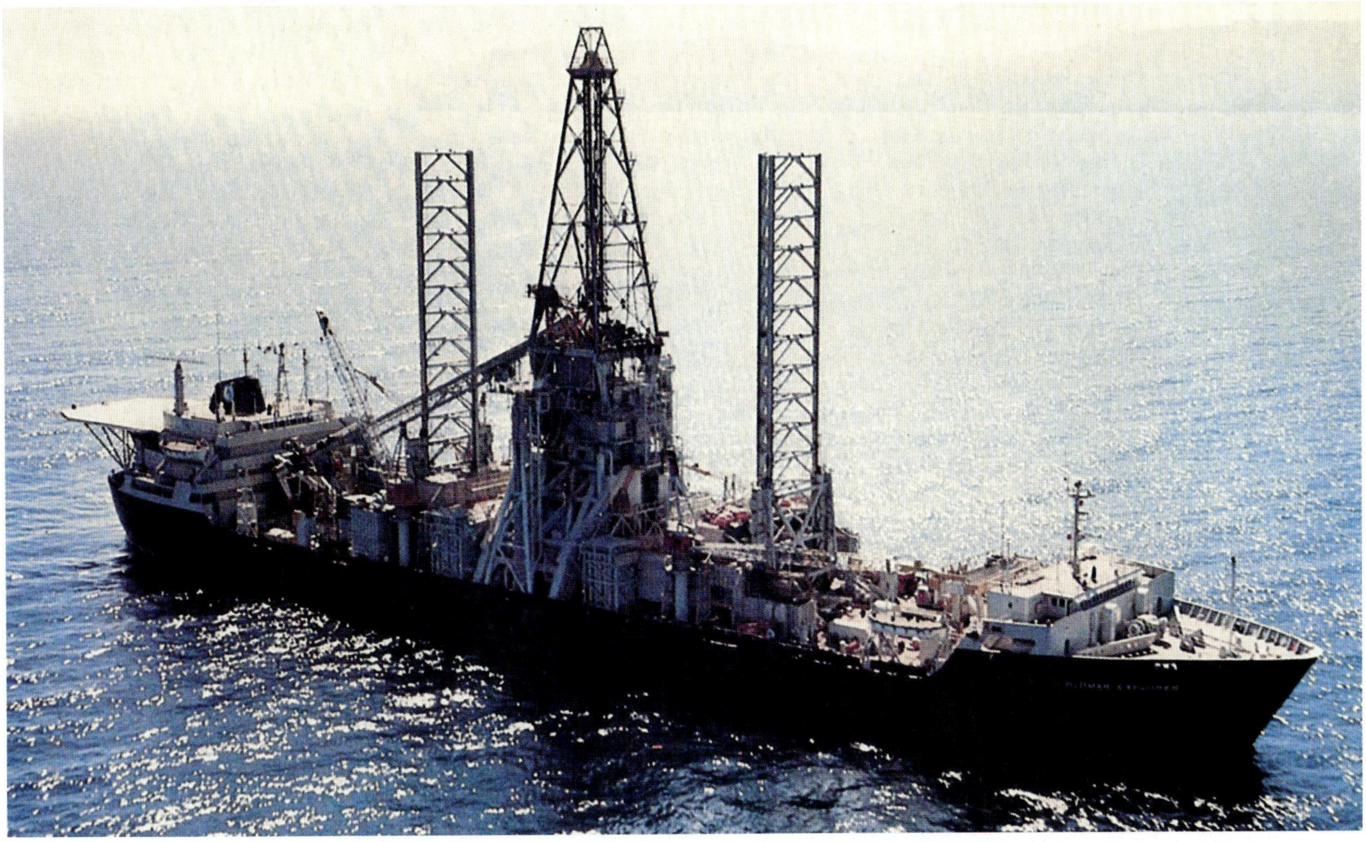

Hunter Killer Subs

The New Capital Ships

RIGHT: The USS *Los Angeles* underway during her sea trials off the Atlantic coast in the summer of 1976 as the NATO build-up of nuclear-powered hunter-killer submarines gained momentum. (US NAVY)

After the USS *Nautilus* set sail on January 17, 1955, its first commanding officer, Eugene P. Wilkinson, signalled the historic message, "underway on nuclear power."

Three years later the power and potential of nuclear-powered submarines was graphically demonstrated when the USS *Nautilus* sailed under the Arctic ice cap at the North Pole.

For the US and British naval chiefs, the arrival of nuclear-powered submarines offered an important weapon to counter the Soviet Union's growing and more capable fleet of submarines.

This was major change from the Battle of the Atlantic when escort vessels and maritime patrol aircraft led the way in defeating the German U-boats. Now, allied submarines would lead the way in finding, tracking, and identifying Soviet submarines.

Hand-in-hand with the development of nuclear reactors to generate power, allied submarines were soon fitted with osmosis technology to produce fresh water and oxygen generators to produce unlimited supplies of air. The 1950s and 1960s also saw major advances in sonar technologies allowing submarines to detect underwater targets at hundreds of miles distance. The days of submarines having to surface to find targets with a periscope appeared to be over.

To complete the underwater arsenal of nuclear-powered submarines, in the 1950s the first homing torpedoes were fielded. These detected the sound of targets and then automatically guided the torpedo towards them. It was now theoretically possible for submarines to conduct patrols without ever having to surface until their return to base.

RIGHT: Crewmen monitoring consoles at the diving station aboard a US Navy Los Angeles class submarine. (US NAVY)

ABOVE: The USS *Nautilus*, the world's first nuclear-powered submarine, during her initial sea trials in January 1955. (US NAVY)

At this time, the increasing use of allied submarines to hunt their Soviet counterparts led to the use of the terms 'hunter-killer' or 'attack' submarines coming into widespread use. They were usually termed SSNs. The era of submarines waging an underwater duel had arrived.

When the first Soviet nuclear-powered submarines appeared in the 1950s, their speed was far in excess of conventionally powered Western submarines of the time. This meant that Soviet nuclear-powered boats would be able speed away from any allied submarine that tried to intercept them.

At a stroke, the Soviets appeared on the verge of making the bulk of the allied submarine fleets, which were still predominately diesel powered, obsolete. Britain and the United States launched crash programmes to

LEFT: The British nuclear-powered attack submarine HMS *Valiant* was commissioned in 1966 and saw active service until 1994, including taking part in the 1982 Falklands conflict. (US NAVY)

rapidly expand their fleets of nuclear attack boats. Older and less capable conventional submarines were retired and by the early 1970s several dozens of nuclear attack submarines were in service with the US Navy and the Royal Navy.

Huge amounts of money were poured into building nuclear submarines. The United States provided Britain with a Westinghouse 5SW reactor to help it launch its first nuclear powered boat, HMS *Dreadnought*, in 1960. Her reactor went critical in the then Vickers Armstrong yard in Barrow-in-Furness in November 1962. She sailed a month later and brought the Royal Navy into the nuclear age. Over the next two decades, the Royal Navy received 11 more boats of the Valiant, Warspite, Swiftsure, and Churchill classes, as well as four Resolution-class ballistic »

LEFT: The USS *Nautilus*, the world's first nuclear powered submarine is open to the public at Groton's Submarine Force Library and Museum. It attracts some 250,000 visitors annually. (US NAVY)

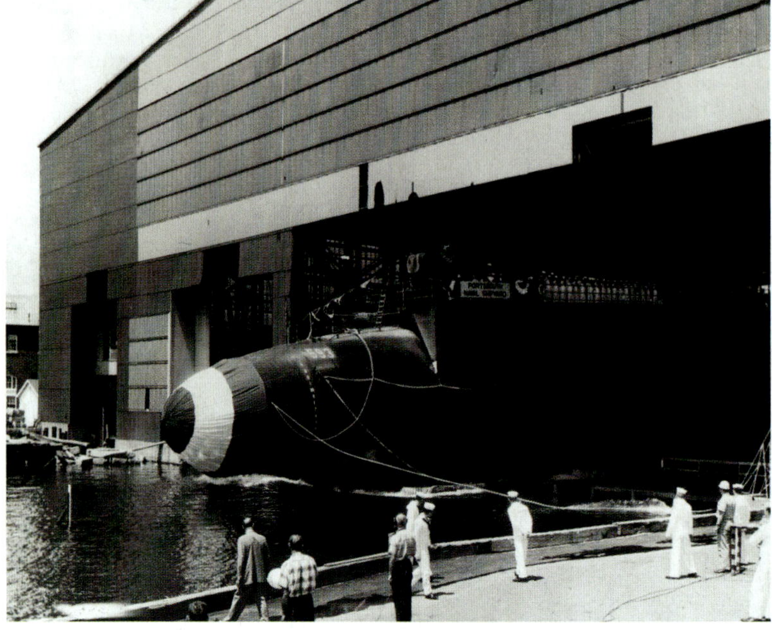

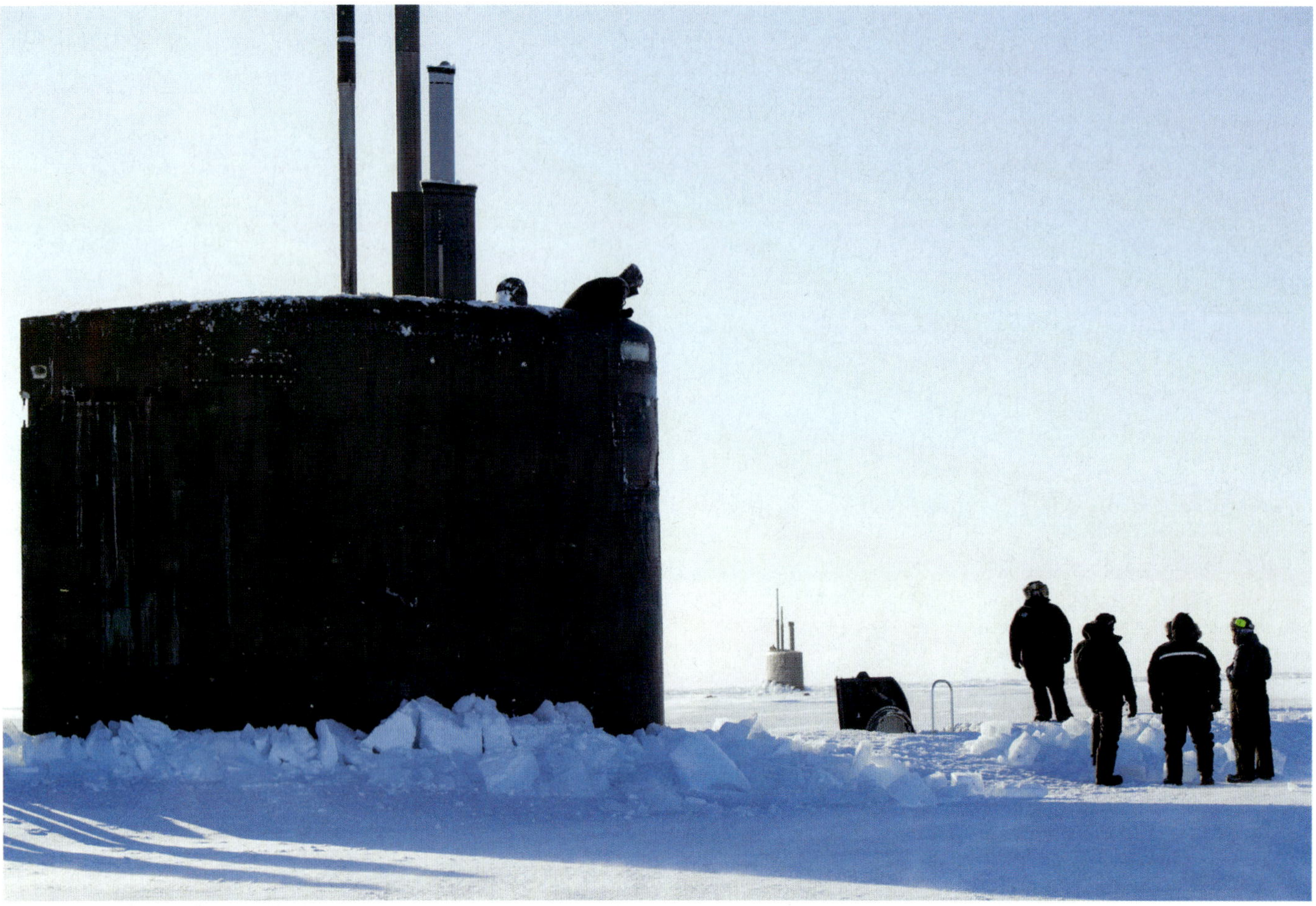

ABOVE: Nuclear submarines now routinely surface at the North Pole to demonstrate their ability to operate under the Arctic ice pack. (US NAVY)

missile firing nuclear powered submarines, or SSBNs.

The US Navy led the way in terms of numbers, building five main classes of nuclear attack submarines between 1955 and the early 1980s. Skate, Skipjack, Permit, Sturgeon, and Los Angeles class attack submarines were put in the water. The demand was so great that the centres of the US nuclear submarine industry at Newport News Shipbuilding in Virginia and General Dynamics Electric Boat at Groton, Connecticut, could not cope. Nuclear attack submarines had to be built at Fore River Shipyard, Mare Island Naval Shipyard, Ingalls Shipbuilding, Portsmouth Naval Shipyard, and New York Shipbuilding. Before the middle of the 1980s, the US Navy had more than 80 nuclear attack submarines in service.

As more and more nuclear attack boats started to come online in the 1960s, US and British submarine commands looked to use them aggressively to dominate the North Atlantic. Their superior speed meant the American and British boats could now outrun their Soviet counterparts. And, when it came to their acoustic signature, the Western submarines were significantly quieter than Soviet equivalents. As a result, American and British nuclear attack submarine captains could run rings around the Soviet navy.

In the Cold War underwater stand-off, the prize was intelligence about an opponent's technology, equipment, and intentions. As the Western nuclear-powered submarines were quieter than their rivals, the Americans and British were able to penetrate deep into Soviet home waters around Murmansk to gather intelligence on their adversary. The two navies' submarine commands divided up their work and established rotas of submarine patrols, so boats were always on station at entrances to main Soviet submarine bases on the Kola peninsula to detect and then track Soviet boats as they left harbour. A high priority was monitoring the trials of new Soviet submarines in a bid to detect new features and capabilities.

British and American submarine captains made daring penetrations into Soviet waters to pick up intelligence, including taking

RIGHT: The launch of USS *Thresher* at the Portsmouth Naval Shipyard, New Hampshire, on July 9, 1960, as the US Navy was ramping up nuclear submarine production. (US NAVY)

underwater photographs of Soviet warships and submarines. In at least one instance, a British submarine snared a Soviet towed sonar array and brought it back to base for examination. However, a handful of American and British submarines suffered damaged in collisions with Soviet submarines and warships.

As Soviet submarines pressed on out into the North Atlantic, the US Navy SOSUS underwater detection network would take over tracking responsibilities. A line of submarine patrol boxes was set up by the Americans and British to cover the line of the Greenland-Iceland-UK, or GIUK, Gap. Once the Soviet vessel had crossed that line the Western boats would reengage and follow the Soviet submarines to make sure they did not get too close to British and US SSBN patrol areas. A key priority was to track any Soviet submarines heading to the vicinity of the Clyde estuary, where the British and Americans had bases for SSBNs.

Aside from occasional bumps and scrapes, this underwater duel was conducted with discretion and professionalism. Neither side wanted to start World War Three. All crews involved were long serving submariners and realised that an accident for either side could result at worse in the sudden death of all involved. At best, damage to multi-million-dollar submarines and serious professional embarrassment that could be career ending.

Despite rapid advances in submarine technology during the

Cold War it was clearly the case that every participant was pushing the boundaries of the possible. Every class of nuclear-powered submarine was better armed, more capable, and reliable than its predecessor as navies and shipyards received feedback from the crews who took them to sea.

The 1982 Falklands conflict showed there were still problems getting homing torpedoes to work. So, when Chris Wreford-Brown, the commanding officer of HMS *Conqueror*, attacked and sank the Argentine cruiser, ARA *General Belgrano*, he elected to fire World War Two-era Mark 8 unguided torpedoes,

instead of the more modern Tigerfish homing weapons. He just did not consider the new torpedo to reliable enough to do the job properly. A day earlier, the Argentine submarine, ARA *San Lois,* has fired two German made SST-4 wire- guided torpedoes at two British frigates. One failed to leave its tube and the other's control wire broke and got nowhere near its targets.

Submarine technology had come a long war following World War Two, but the underwater weapons of the Cold War were still in many cases not really mature and needed further development.

ABOVE: Mark 48 homing torpedoes entered US Navy service from 1972 and allowed US hunter-killer submarines to engage Russian submarines at extreme depths. It can be guided via command wires from the launch submarine or on-board sonar sensors in the front of the torpedo. (US NAVY)

BELOW: Up to 1968, 14 Thresher-class nuclear powered attack submarines were built. The lead boat, USS *Thresher*, was lost with all hands during trials in April 1963. (US NAVY)

Cold War Warriors

Anti-Submarine Frigates

RIGHT: An Ikara missile is test fired from HMAS *Stuart* off the New South Wales coast in 1988. The weapon was designed to project a torpedo up to 19 kilometres from the launch ship. (MONGRELDOG)

BELOW: The 1970s saw the widespread fielding of the first anti-submarine frigates equipped to operate small helicopters. HMS *Apollo*, a Royal Navy Leader-class frigate entered service in 1972. (ROYAL NAVY)

At the height of the Battle of the Atlantic, Royal Navy and allied convoy escort vessels began to hunt down German U-boats with hull-mounted sonar and depth charges. When Soviet nuclear-powered submarines started to appear in the late 1950s, they rendered World War Two era anti-submarine technology obsolete.

Western navies had to redesign their anti-submarine frigates so they could find Soviet submarines at long ranges and engage them before they had a chance to open fire with torpedoes or anti-ship cruise missiles. The expectation that some of those Soviet cruise missiles might have nuclear warheads made it even more imperative that hostile submarines be neutralised long before they had the chance to get off the first shot.

Firstly, future NATO anti-submarine frigates needed to be faster, and more agile, than Soviet submarines. So, from the late 1950s they started to feature gas turbines that could generate full speed in a few seconds, rather than requiring several hours to build up speed.

The performance of sonar technology was improved to identify and track hostile submarines at longer range. World War Two era warships mounted their sonar in their bow to give them good forward coverage as they closed in on U-boats. But bow-mounted sonars resulted in a blind spot appearing in the vessel's aft sector, due to turbulence from its propeller and the flow behind it. This could potentially allow an opposing submarine to approach undetected behind warships and position themselves for a torpedo shot from close range.

Cold War era sub-hunting warships had to be optimised to find and track submarines across 360° to prevent surprise attack. The answer was what is usually called a towed array sonar, which incorporated hydro-phones attached to several hundred metres of cable. These are reeled out behind

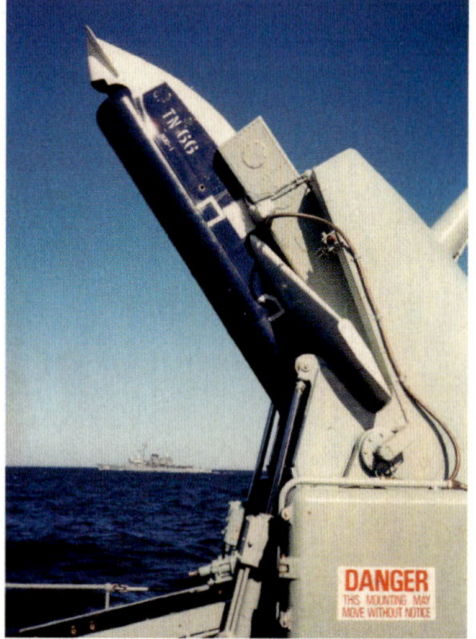

a warship and move the sonar safely away from the turbulence caused by a warship's own propellers.

Through the early 1960s the US Navy conducted a series of experiments with both nuclear-powered submarines and surface

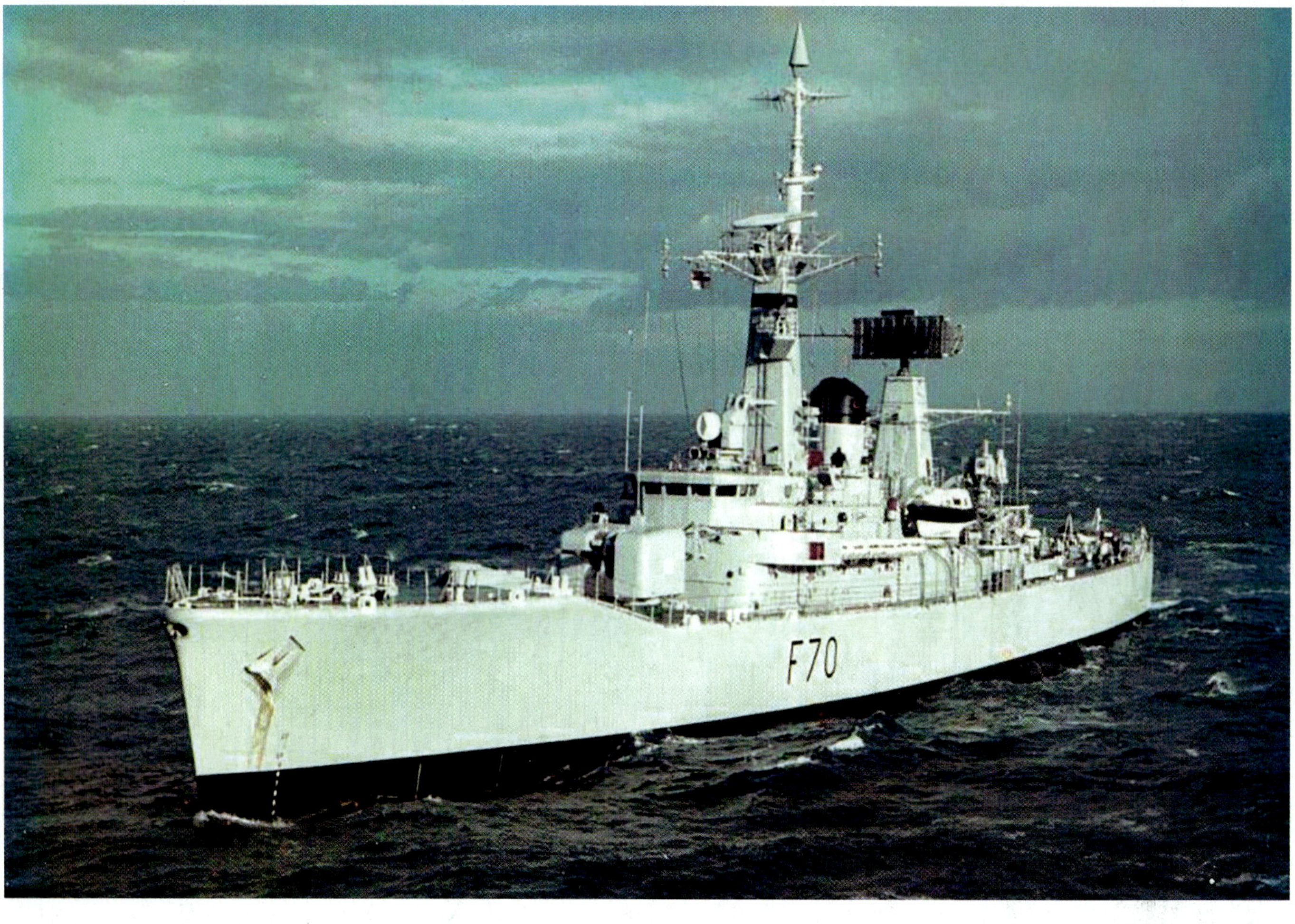

vessels, with tests culminating in 1964-1965 with the detection of a submarine at 60 nautical miles. These led to the tender for the AN/SQR-14 towed array in 1967, and the deployment in 1970 of three systems on US warships operating in the Mediterranean.

As towed array technology became more mature, they became able to detect submarines at hundreds of nautical miles range.

To kill submarines at long range, anti-submarine vessels were equipped with deck-mounted launchers for homing torpedoes. In the 1960s, the Royal Navy and US Navy developed rocket assisted torpedoes that could project these weapons over 10km from the launch vessel. The US RUR-5 ASROC, for 'Anti-Submarine Rocket', and British Ikara were fitted to a wide array of vessels but were not considered to be a very effective or reliable.

The real transformative development was the conversion of frigate-sized warships to carry helicopters, armed with depth charges and homing torpedoes. When these helicopters were fitted with dipping sonars or sonobuoys, they could start to hunt down hostile submarines on their own rather than just drop their weapons on the orders of their parent warship.

ABOVE: The British Leander-class frigate HMS *Naiad* underway on NATO anti-submarine exercises in the North Atlantic in 1981. The tail of her Wasp helicopter can just be made out on deck. (US NAVY)

LEFT: French navy Georges Leygues-class frigates were fitted with DUBV43 towed sonar arrays in the 1970s. (JEAN-MICHEL ROCHE)

Anti-Submarine Helicopters

The New Sub-Hunters

W hen helicopters started to enter widespread use with NATO navies in the 1950s, their potential for anti-submarine operations was immediately recognised.

The ability of helicopters to land and take off vertically meant that they could operate from frigate-sized vessels fitted with a flight deck. Bigger frigates could also be designed to incorporate a hangar, so embarked helicopters could be protected from bad weather when not flying. This was essential to allow the prolonged helicopter operations at sea from small warships. These helicopters had to be designed with folding blades and tail booms, to allow them to be fitted inside ship's hangars.

Landing on a moving warship's deck required a skilled pilot, often with strong nerves. Once on deck, helicopters risked rolling or being washed overboard in very stormy weather. So clamping mechanising were fitted to some helicopters to allow their pilots to secure their machines on flight decks before shutting down their engines.

Helicopter technology advanced rapidly and, in the 1950s and 1960s, they became increasingly more reliable and capable.

The first generation of anti-submarine helicopters, such as the British Westland Wasp, were ordered in 1961 to fill the Royal Navy's 'Manned Torpedo-Carrying Helicopter' (MATCH) requirement. It had no sensors and was simply a 'truck' to carry torpedoes or depth charges. These were dropped on the orders of controllers in the helicopter's parent ship.

Sikorsky in America fielded the S-58 in the 1950s and it was the first helicopter to enter service with a dipping sonar, so it could hunt submarines on its own.

It was licence built in Britain as the Wessex for the Royal Navy. The S-58 was known in US Navy service as the SH-34G/H or HSS Seabat. Although the ability to hunt submarines from a hovering helicopter was a major advance, these early helicopters did not have the performance to both carry a dipping sonar and anti-submarine weapons. Radars were eventually fitted to the helicopters to give them the ability to detect submarine periscopes or snorkels.

In 1957 the US Navy awarded a contract to begin the development of the helicopter that eventually became known as the iconic SH-3 Sea King. The helicopter was to

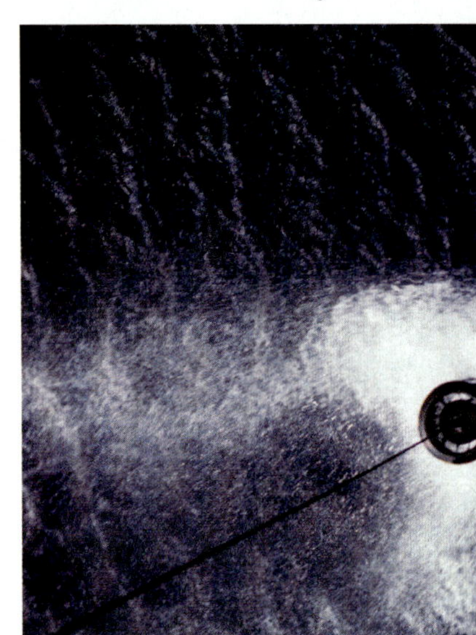

have turbo-shaft engines that gave it dramatically improved performance over the Wessex, so it could carry both dipping sonar and weapons. It also had a distinctive boat shaped hull so could, in theory, land on the sea to recover people or make a controlled landing if the helicopter suffered a mishap.

The mighty Sea King first flew in 1959 and entered US Navy service in 1961. Licenced production took place in Canada, Italy, Japan, and Britain. The US Navy's Sea Kings remained in use until 2006 but many other navies still operate them. In total more than 1,300 were built around the world and the type perhaps became most recognised when they were used to recover Apollo astronauts after the capsules splashed down following moon landing missions.

During its operational life, the US Navy and allied navies progressively updated the Sea King, adding improved sensors, weapons, and communications systems. The most capable, anti-submarine versions of the iconic Sea King were the HAS5 and HAS6 variants built by Westland for the Royal Navy in the 1980s. These versions boasted acoustic processing systems similar to those found in fixed wing maritime patrol aircraft so they could sow, and then control large fields of sonobuoys. These helicopters were also some of the first to be equipped with data links to allow the automatic sharing of tactical information around naval task groups.

Royal Navy Sea King HAS5s saw action in the 1982 Falklands conflict and were the only anti-submarine helicopters to date to use homing torpedoes and depth charges in action for real. Their prey, an Argentine Type 209 diesel submarine, escaped them.

Although the most capable anti-submarine helicopter of its era, »

ABOVE: A Sikorsky SH-34G/H or Seabat from US Navy Reserve Helicopter Anti-submarine Squadron HS-831 employs its dipping sonar during an exercise in 1960. (US NAVY)

LEFT: The Royal Navy's Westland Wasp HAS1 was introduced from 1963 and served aboard small anti-submarine frigates for 25 years. It had no sensors to hunt submarines and just dropped torpedoes on instructions from controllers on the helicopter's parent ship. (AIRWOLFHOUND)

ABOVE: A US Navy SH-3H Sea King from Helicopter Anti-Submarine Squadron HS-12 in the service's distinctive 1970s colour scheme. (US NAVY)

WESTLAND SEA KING HAS5

Crew:	Two to four
Length:	55ft 10in (17.02m)
Height:	16ft 10in (5.13m)
Max take-off weight:	21,400lb (9,707kg)
Powerplant:	Two × Rolls-Royce H.1400-2 Gnome turboshaft engines
Cruise speed:	112kts (129mph, 207kph)
Range:	664nm (764 miles, 1,230km)
Armament:	
Four × Mark 44, Mark 46, or Sting Ray torpedoes, or four × depth charges	
Provision for a door mounted machine gun	

the Sea King was just too big to be routinely embarked on frigate-sized warships. Through the 1970s and into the 1980s, they were provided with a new generation of smaller maritime helicopters that offered greater anti-submarine capability than those first machines from the early 1960s. The Royal Navy started to field the Westland Lynx in the 1970s and it featured an improved surface surveillance radar that could spot snorkels and periscopes, as well as the ability to drop homing torpedoes and depth charges. Westland also offered customers a version with a dipping sonar, but the Royal Navy did not take this up.

The US Navy, at the same time was looking to field its own new small maritime helicopter on its frigates and destroyers. It selected a version of the Sikorsky UH-60 Blackhawk, which it dubbed the SH-60B Seahawk, Light Airborne Multi-Purpose System (LAMPS) Mark IIII. This had the ability to deploy and control sonobuoys, as well as a magnetic anomaly detector, or MAD. These systems allowed US Navy SH-60B crews to duel with Soviet submarines at depth. Cramming so much equipment into a small helicopter proved a challenge and it took more than six years to make it all work

together effectively. The first Seahawk saw frontline service in 1985.

Naval helicopters of the 1980s were far more capable and reliable aircraft than their forefathers from the 1950s. By the 1980s it was routine for every NATO anti-submarine frigate to operate a helicopter to vastly extend the amount of sea space they could dominate. The design of these ships now revolved around making helicopter operations as efficient as possible. Ships, helicopters, sensors, and weapons were all designed from the start to be part of an integrated anti-submarine weapon of war.

RIGHT: A US Navy anti-submarine operator monitors the AN/AQS-13 dipping sonar control panel inside an SH-3H Sea King helicopter. (US NAVY)

Lockheed's Neptune

God of the Sea

At the height of World War Two, the US Navy contracted Lockheed to design a purpose-built anti-submarine aircraft to take the war to the U-boats. The result was the P-2 Neptune, or P2V as it was known the United States Navy up to 1962. It was named after the Roman god of the sea and established a US Navy tradition of naming its maritime patrol aircraft after figures from the classical world, which continues to this day.

The twin piston-engined aircraft was envisaged as being cheap and easy to manufacture. A prototype first flew in May 1945 just as Nazi Germany was surrendering, but the US Navy was still keen to replace its assortment of patrol aircraft with a more modern land-based type.

It was optimised to counter the snorkel equipped U-boats that the Germans were fielding in the latter part of World War Two, with a powerful radar to detect periscopes and snorkels at a distance and magnetic anomaly detector (MAD) to localise the position of a submarine. Neptunes were armed with rockets, bombs, and depth charges to strike and destroy submarines near the surface.

The Neptune was one of the first aircraft to be equipped to use sonobuoys that could be used to detect submarines underwater. Sonobuoys used acoustic signals to pick up the noise from submarines and then transmitted the results up to the controlling aircraft. These early sonobuoys were controlled manually by operators in the Neptune, who had to calculate a submarine's position using slide rules and paper charts.

Over its life the Neptune proved a rugged and dependable aircraft, but it was of its era and lacked the modern systems to track nuclear submarines successfully.

Eventually 1,117 Neptunes were built by Lockheed and its partner in Japan. Ten allied air forces ended up operating the Neptune and they remained in service into the 1980s.

LEFT: The Lockheed P2V-7 Neptune was the US Navy and NATO's most numerous anti-submarine aircraft in the 1950s and early 1960s. Here an aircraft of US Navy patrol squadron VP-56 operates in South American waters during Exercise Unitas IV in August 1963. (US NAVY)

BELOW: The Royal Netherlands Navy operated Lockheed P2V-7B, P-2H, and SP-2H aircraft from 1953 to 1982. (INSTITUUT VOOR MARITIEME HISTORIE)

LOCKHEED P-2H / P2V-7 NEPTUNE

Crew: Seven to nine

Length: 27.94m (91ft 8in)

Wingspan: 31.65m (103ft 10in)

Height: 8.94m (29ft 4in)

Max take-off weight: 36,240kg (79,895lb)

Powerplant: Two × Wright R-3350-32W Duplex-Cyclone radial piston engines (later versions fitted with two × Westinghouse J34-WE-34 turbojet engines)

Maximum speed: 584kph (315kts)

Range: 3,471km (1,874nm)

Armament:

Rockets: 2.75in FFAR in removable wing-mounted pods

Bombs: 8,000lb (3,629kg) including free-fall bombs, depth charges, and torpedoes

Avro Shackleton

The Growler

AVRO SHACKLETON	
Crew: Ten	
Length: 26.62m (87ft 4in)	
Wingspan: 37m (120ft)	
Height: 17ft 6in (5.33m)	
Max take-off weight: 39,009kg (86,000lb)	
Powerplant: Four × Rolls-Royce Griffon 57 V-12 liquid-cooled piston engines	
Maximum speed: 300mph (260kts)	
Range: 2,240 miles (3,610km)	
Endurance: 14 hours 36 minutes	
Armament:	
Guns: Two × 20mm Hispano Mark V cannon in the nose	
Bombs: 10,000lb of bombs, torpedoes, mines, or conventional or nuclear depth charges, including the Mk 101 Lulu	

ABOVE: The business end of a South African Air Force Avro Shackleton MR3. Its twin Hispano-Suiza HS.404 cannons were intended to engage surfaced submarines at long range. (NJR ZA)

For twenty years from 1951, the main maritime patrol aircraft of the Royal Air Force was the Avro Shackleton.

Its heritage stretched back to Avro's Lancaster bomber and the Shackleton retained the general shape of the iconic World War Two workhorse, including its twin tails. The Shackleton was powered by four Rolls-Royce Griffon 57 engines and had distinctive counter-rotating propellers. Eventually 185 Shackletons were built, including eight for the South African Air Force.

Design work on the Shackleton began in the final days of World War Two and it drew heavily on the lessons of the Battle of the Atlantic. It was optimised for detecting and attacking submarines on the surface or at periscope depth. It had two 20mm Hispano cannons in the nose to engage submarines on the surface and had a powerful surveillance radar to find targets at night.

The Shackleton was equipped with early generation sonobuoys to detect submarines underwater, but these used analogue technology and operators had control them individually.

RAF Shackleton squadrons operated across the world in the final days of the British empire, from the Caribbean to Gibraltar and Malta in the Mediterranean, Aden and Sharjah in the Middle East, Gan in the Indian Ocean, and Singapore in the Far East.

Although popular with its crews, the Shackleton was notoriously unreliable and the MR3 variant had poor stall capabilities. It was also very noisy, leading to its crews nicknaming it the 'Growler'. The final maritime patrol aircraft were retired from RAF service in 1971 but 12 were converted into airborne early warning aircraft and remained on duty for another 20 years.

RIGHT: An RAF Shackleton MR2 of 224 Squadron flying in formation near Masirah Airbase in Oman in 1958. (COL SMILEY)

Breguet Atlantic

Europe's Sub Hunter

When NATO looked to boost its anti-submarine capabilities in the late 1950s a multi-national programme was launched to build a new maritime patrol aircraft.

A design by the French company, Breguet, won the order and a consortium, dubbed Société d'Étude et de Construction de Breguet Atlantic (SECBAT), was formed to build the Atlantic at Toulouse in France.

Unlike its contemporaries, the Lockheed P-3 Orion and Hawker Siddeley Nimrod, the Atlantic was purpose designed for maritime patrol rather than being based on an existing airliner. The Atlantic was designed to carry either eight guided torpedoes or 12 depth charges, or two AM.39 Exocet anti-ship missiles in its internal bomb bay.

The first orders were placed in 1963, with France buying 40 and Germany said it would buy 20. NATO allies, the Netherland and Italy also bought the aircraft and Pakistan subsequently received second hand aircraft from France.

The Atlantic was delivered with a first-generation acoustic system to allow crews to use sonobuoys to track submarines under water.

By the 1980s, the Atlantic's systems were reaching obsolescence, and an upgrade programme was launched to incorporate fully digital acoustic

BREGUET ATLANTIC
Crew: 12
Length: 31.62m (103ft 9in)
Wingspan: 37.42m (122ft 9in) including wingtip pods
Height: 10.89m (35ft 9in)
Max take-off weight: 46,200kg (101,854lb)
Powerplant: Two × Rolls-Royce Tyne RTy.20 Mk 21 2-spool turboprop engines
Cruise speed: 315kph (196mph, 170kts) patrol speed
Endurance: 18 hours
Armament:
Up to 3,500kg (7,700lb), including torpedoes, depth charges, mines, anti-ship missiles, bombs, and/or buoys

ABOVE: The Royal Netherlands Navy operated nine Breguet BR1150 Atlantic in the 1970s and early 1980s until they were replaced by P-3 Orions. (KONINKLIJKE MARINE)

systems and improved sensors. In the end, the French Navy was the only air arm to adopt this version, which was officially dubbed the Atlantique 2, but it was also known as the Atlantique Nouvelle Génération or ATL2. Germany, Italy, and the Netherlands all retired their aircraft and replaced them with different types. A further upgrade is underway to allow the French Navy to keep the aircraft in service until 2035.

LEFT: The Breguet Br.1150 Atlantic had a distinctive fuselage profile with a pressurised hull cabin above a weapon bay. The British Nimrod followed this concept. (ADRIAN PINGSTONRE)

P-3 Orion

The Great Hunter

As Soviet nuclear submarine production ramped up in the 1950s, the US Navy decided it needed to boost its ability to find, track and identify its underwater opponents.

A replacement was needed for the Lockheed P-2 Neptune, which had been designed in World War Two, and could not be modified for the new era. In 1957, the US Navy asked America's aviation industry to come up with proposals.

Lockheed offered the US Navy a modified version of its L-188 Electra airliner, which had yet to fly. This reduced development cost, but the choice of an airliner also ensured the new maritime patrol aircraft had plenty of room inside its large cabin to accommodate the complex electronic equipment needed for anti-submarine operations. It also provided the mission crew with the higher level of

US NAVY P-3 ORION MARITIME PATROL (VP) SQUADRONS, 1980				
Unit/Base	**Aircraft Variant**	**Specialist Role**	**Nicknames**	**Location**
US Pacific Fleet				
Patrol and Reconnaissance Wing 2				Naval Air Station Barbers Point, Hawaii
VP-1	P-3B		Screaming Eagles	Naval Air Station Barbers Point, Hawaii
VP-4	P-3B		Skinny Dragons	Naval Air Station Barbers Point, Hawaii
VP-6	P-3B		Blue Sharks	Naval Air Station Barbers Point, Hawaii
VP-17	P-3B		White Lightnings	Naval Air Station Barbers Point, Hawaii
VP-22			Blue Geese	Naval Air Station Barbers Point, Hawaii
Patrol and Reconnaissance Wing 10				Naval Air Station Moffett Field, California
VP-9	P-3C		Golden Eagles	Naval Air Station Moffett Field, California
VP-19	P-3C		Big Red	Naval Air Station Moffett Field, California
VP-31	P-3B/C	Fleet Replenishment/ Training	Black Lightnings	Naval Air Station Moffett Field, California
VP-40	P-3C		Fighting Marlins	Naval Air Station Moffett Field, California
VP-46	P-3C		Gray Knights	Naval Air Station Moffett Field, California
VP-47	P-3C		Golden Swordsmen	Naval Air Station Moffett Field, California
VP-48	P-3C		Boomers	Naval Air Station Moffett Field, California
VP-50	P-3C		Blue Dragons	Naval Air Station Moffett Field, California
Reserve Patrol Wing Pacific				NAS Moffett Field, California
VP 60	P-3A		Cobras	NAS Glenview, Illinois
VP 65	P-3A		Tridents	NAS Point Mugu, California
VP-67	P-3A		Golden Hawks	Naval Air Station Memphis, Tennessee
VP-69	P-3A		Totems	NAS Whidbey Island, Washington
VP-90	P-3A		Lions	NAS Glenview, Illinois
VP-91	P-3B		Stingers / Black Cats	NAS Moffett Field, California

US NAVY P-3 ORION MARITIME PATROL (VP) SQUADRONS, 1980

Unit/Base	Aircraft Variant	Specialist Role	Nicknames	Location
US Atlantic Fleet				
Patrol and Reconnaissance Wing 11				Naval Air Station Jacksonville, Florida
VP-5	P-3C		Mad Foxes	Naval Air Station Jacksonville, Florida
VP-16	P-3C		War Eagles	Naval Air Station Jacksonville, Florida
VP-24	P-3C		Batmen	Naval Air Station Jacksonville, Florida
VP-30	P-3A/B/C	Fleet Replenishment/ Training	Pro's Nest	Naval Air Station Jacksonville, Florida
VP-45	P-3C		Pelicans	Naval Air Station Jacksonville, Florida
VP-49	P-3C		Woodpeckers	Naval Air Station Jacksonville, Florida
VP-56	P-3C		Dragons	Naval Air Station Jacksonville, Florida
Patrol and Reconnaissance Wing 5				Naval Air Station Brunswick, Maine
VP-8	P-3B		Tigers	Naval Air Station Brunswick, Maine
VP-10	P-3B		Red Lancers	Naval Air Station Brunswick, Maine
VP-11	P-3B		Pegasus	Naval Air Station Brunswick, Maine
VP-23	P-3B		Sea Hawks	Naval Air Station Brunswick, Maine
VP-26	P-3B		Tridents	Naval Air Station Brunswick, Maine
VP-44	P-3C		Golden Pelicans	Naval Air Station Brunswick, Maine
Reserve Patrol Wing Atlantic				NAS Norfolk, Virginia
VP-62	P-3A		Broadarrows	Naval Air Station Jacksonville, Florida
VP-64	P-3A		Condors	Naval Air Station Willow Grove, Pennsylvania
VP-66	P-3A		Liberty Bells	Naval Air Station Willow Grove, Pennsylvania
VP-68	P-3A		Blackhawks	Naval Air Station Patuxent River, Maryland
VP-92	P-3A		Minutemen	NAS South Weymouth, Massachusetts
VP-93	P-3A		Executioners	NAF Detroit/Selfridge ANGB, Michigan
VP-94	P-3A		Crawfishers	NAS Belle Chase, Louisiana

comfort needed to effectively operate this complex equipment.

The US Navy's sub-hunter was not a complete break with the past. There was still a need to make rapid dive attacks on submarines on or close to the surface, so the Orion's airframe had to be strengthened to enable it to take the stresses of violent manoeuvres at low altitudes. Extra attention was paid to protecting key components from sea water corrosion caused by prolonged low-level flights over the world's oceans.

The first prototype YP3V-1, as it was then designated, took to the skies in August 1958 and deliveries to the US Navy commenced in 1962. When America and the Soviet Union lurched to the brink of nuclear war during the October 1962 Cuban missile crisis, P-3s got their debut on the world stage trying to enforce President John F. Kennedy's 'quarantine' of the Caribbean island.

In 1962, the US military changed its aircraft designation system, and the Orion became the P-3, just as production was ramping up at Lockheed's Burbank plant in California. Production continued at the site until 1991 and then moved to Marietta in Georgia to complete the final export order to South Korea. In total 650 P-3s were built by Lockheed and 107 were licence built by Kawasaki in Japan, with its final aircraft being delivered in 2000 bringing an end to 38 years of Orion production.

After it became the main US Navy maritime patrol aircraft during the 1960s, the Orion became a familiar visitor to NATO and allied airbases around the world. It was immediately recognisable from its four turbo-propellers, distinctive wing shape, and long magnetic anomaly detector (MAD) boom under its tail.

The Orion incorporated all the essential features of a maritime patrol aircraft of its era. A bomb bay could accommodate depth charges or homing torpedoes. More weapons could be carried on underwing pylons, including AGM-84 Harpoon »

LEFT: P-3C Orion aircraft from the navies of the Japan Maritime Self-Defense Force, Canada, Australia, Republic of Korea, and the US line the Rainbow Fleet tarmac of Marine Corps Air Station Kaneohe Bay during the Rim of the Pacific (RIMPAC) 2010 exercise. (US NAVY)

BELOW: Production of P-3 Orions took place at Lockheed's Burbank plant in California for more than thirty years until 1991. (US NAVY/LOCKHEED MARTIN)

ABOVE: An underside view of a P-3C Orion showing the magnetic anomaly detector -the boom at the rear of the airplane - and the sonar buoy launchers - the grid of dark spots towards the rear of the fuselage. (MARK WAGNER)

anti-ship missiles. It had a surface surveillance radar to look for ships, but it was optimised to detect submarine conning towers, periscopes, or snorkels. Sonobuoys to detect and track underwater submarines were dispensed via fuselage launchers just behind the wings.

Externally the Orion's appearance did not change much during its life, but the aircraft's sub-hunting capabilities were transformed by major upgrades to its mission systems and sensors. During the first 30 years of its US Navy service, major investments were made to its acoustic systems to enable P-3 crews to detect and then maintain tracks of nuclear submarines underwater.

There were three variants of the aircraft, as well five major upgrade projects and numerous minor modifications up to 1990 when the fall of the Berlin Wall led the US Navy to halt upgrade work on the aircraft's anti-submarine capabilities. The threat had evaporated overnight.

The P-3 has the distinction of being the first maritime patrol aircraft to incorporate a fully blown computer. This was designed to help the operators analyse the information from the aircraft's sonobuoys and then display tactical information on a single screen. As computing power grew, then new computers were progressively installed. This allowed more and more sonobuoys to be simultaneously controlled, dramatically increasing the area of sea that could be monitored.

RIGHT: The Royal Canadian Air Force bought 21 Lockheed CP-140 Aurora variants in 1979, which featured a bespoke mission system to suit the service's unique requirements. (ARCTURUS)

In three decades, the Orion cabin areas had been transformed. In 1962 when the first P-3As had been delivered, the crew operated a series of stand-alone analogue sensor stations. By the mid 1980s, the cabin contained a series of computerised work stations, that automatically displayed tactical information.

The analysis of the acoustic data generated by the sonobuoys was also automated to ease the work load of operators so submarine track information could be rapidly incorporated in the P-3's master tactical plot. A new generation of sonobuoys were fielded on the P-3, which could detect and track submarines at greater distances and in a greater number of sea conditions. As quieter Soviet submarines appeared in the 1970s and 1980s, more capable sonobuoys were needed to detect them.

Key Asset

In the great duel between the US Navy anti-submarine forces and the Soviet nuclear submarine fleet, the P-3 was a key element. Its mission systems and sensors could be upgraded at a fraction of the cost of making changes to nuclear-powered attack submarines. So, the P-3 fleet was often the first part of the US Navy anti-submarine response that was able to stay ahead of the Soviets.

At its peak, the Orion was operated by seven NATO air arms and another eight air forces around the world bought the aircraft. It remains in service with 11 air forces.

The US launched a number of efforts in the 1990s to replace the Orion as its aircraft began to be impacted by the long term effects of intensive use and corrosion. An eight year-long process to introduce the successor, the Boeing P-8 Poseidon, into the US Navy began in 2012. Orion's soldiered on until May 2020 when the final US Navy maritime patrol squadron retired its last P-3C.

LOCKHEED P-3C ORION	
Crew: 11	
Length: 35.61m (116ft 10in)	
Wingspan: 30.38m (99ft 8in)	
Height: 10.27m (33ft 8.5in)	
Max take-off weight: 61,235kg (135,000lb)	
Powerplant: Four × Allison T56-A-14 turboprop engines	
Cruise speed: 607kph (328kts)	
Combat range: 2,491km (1,345nm)	
Endurance: 17 hours	
Armament:	
Ten wing stations in total (three on each wing and two on each wing root) and eight internal bomb bay stations, with provisions to carry combinations of:	
Missiles:	
AGM-65 Maverick, AGM-84 Harpoon, 4×AGM-84 SLAM-ER	
Bombs/Depth Charges:	
Mk 101 Lulu nuclear depth bomb, Mk20 Rockeye, Mk80 Series (Mk82, Mk83, Mk84) general-purpose bombs, B57 nuclear bomb	
Torpedoes:	
Mk 44 , Mk 46, Mk 50, Mk 54, MU90 Impact torpedoes	
Naval mines: various	

A handful of specialist test and trial variants, as well as the EP-3E Aries II signals intelligence aircraft, still remain in service with the US Navy. They are all expected to be retired by 2025.

In its long operational life, the P-3 Orion was the first maritime patrol aircraft to bring airborne sub-hunting into the computer era. In the game of underwater cat and mouse with the Soviet submarine fleet, it gave the West a key advantage.

P-3C UPDATES	
Variant	**Entered Service**
P-3A	July 1962
P-3B	December 1965
P-3C	June 1969
P-3C, Update I	January 1975
P-3C, Update II	August 1977
P-3C, Update II.5	May 1981
P-3C, Update III	January 1985
P-3C, Update III, Retrofit	March 1987
P-3C, Update IV	Cancelled 1992

S-3 Viking

Carrier-borne Sub Hunter

The US Navy launched a competition in the late 1960s to replace the Grumman S-2 Tracker anti-submarine aircraft which were embarked on its aircraft carriers.

Lockheed, in partnership with LTV, won the contract in 1969 to begin building the S-3 Viking. This was to be capable of landing and taking off from aircraft carriers and then hunting submarines with sonobuoys and air dropped homing torpedoes. The idea was for anti-submarine helicopters to provide an inner anti-submarine screen around US Navy

LOCKHEED S-3A VIKING

Crew: Four

Length: 16.26m (53ft 4in)

Wingspan: 20.93m (68ft 8in)

Max take-off weight: 23,831kg (52,539lb)

Powerplant: Two × General Electric TF34-GE-2 turbofan engines

Cruise speed: 650kph (350kts)

Combat range: 853km (460nm)

Armament:

Up to 4,900lb (2,200kg) on four internal and two external hardpoints, for bombs, torpedoes, and depth charges

carrier battle groups and the S-3 would provide the outer-ring.

It had high wings and two large turbo-fan engines, which led to it being nicknamed the 'War Hover'. Serial production lasted for four years from 1974 and resulted in 186 aircraft being built for the US Navy, the type's sole military user.

The S-3 featured a computerised acoustic system to allow the aircraft's four strong crew to operate over extended periods. Its high level of automation allowed the crew to control similar sized sonobuoy fields to the land-based P-3.

The aircraft also had an anti-ship role with AGM-84 Harpoon guided missiles, as well as a secondary air-to-air refuelling role.

With the fall of the Soviet Union in 1991, the Viking's anti-submarine role became redundant, and it was focused on surface or overland surveillance. The type was withdrawn from service on aircraft carriers in 2009, although some remained in non-combat support roles until 2016. A Viking famously flew US President George W Bush onboard the USS *Abraham Lincoln* at the end of the 2003 Iraq war to deliver his 'mission accomplished' speech.

ABOVE: A US Navy S-3A Viking of Anti-Submarine Squadron 31 (VS-31) over the Mediterranean Sea in May 1983 during its cruise embarked on the USS *Dwight D. Eisenhower*. It has its AN/ASQ-81 Magnetic Anomaly Detection (MAD) boom extended from the tail section. (US NAVY)

LEFT: A US Navy S-3B Viking from Sea Control Squadron VS-35 became 'Navy One' when it carried US President George W Bush flew aboard the aircraft carrier USS *Abraham Lincoln* on May 1, 2003. He was the first serving US President to land on an aircraft carrier in an airplane making an arrested landing, while sitting the Viking's co-pilot seat. Controversially, he later declared 'mission accomplished' regarding the Iraq invasion on the deck of the carrier. (US NAVY)

SUBSCRIBE

FlyPast is internationally regarded as the magazine for aviation history and heritage.

shop.keypublishing.com/fpsubs

Britain at War is dedicated to exploring every aspect of the involvement of Britain and her Commonwealth in conflicts from the turn of the 20th century through to the present day.

shop.keypublishing.com/bawsubs

ORDER DIRECT FROM OUR SHOP...

shop.keypublis

OR CALL +44 (0)1780 480404

(Lines open 9.00-5.30, Monday-Friday GMT)

TODAY

Aeroplane is still providing the best aviation coverage around. With focus on iconic military aircraft from the 1930s to the 1960s.

shop.keypublishing.com/amsubs

Aviation News is renowned for providing the best coverage of every branch of aviation.

shop.keypublishing.com/ansubs

hing.com

A little-known chapter in the development of anti-submarine weapons and tactics took place at the height of the Cold War when the US and its allies deployed hundreds of nuclear depth charges to counter the growing Soviet submarine fleet.

At the dawn of the nuclear age, the United States Navy was fascinated by the idea of using atomic bombs to devastate enemy fleets. At the Operation Crossroads atom bomb tests at Bikini Atoll in 1946 an array of vessels was gathered to evaluate the effect of nuclear weapons on them. The target fleet included four obsolete US battleships, two aircraft carriers, two cruisers, 13 destroyers, eight submarines, numerous auxiliary, and amphibious vessels, and three surrendered German and Japanese ships. These included the captured German battle cruiser the *Prinz Eugen*.

The ships and submarines succumbed to blast waves, heat

On the edge of Armageddon

Anti-Submarine Nukes

and tidal waves created by three atom blasts and convinced the US Navy to develop a whole family of nuclear weapons.

By the 1960s, NATO had adopted the strategy of Flexible Response, which envisaged a graduated escalation of a Soviet attack, including the use of 'low yield' tactical nuclear weapons ahead of full exchange of strategic nuclear weapons.

In the naval arena, this led to the deployment of hundreds of Mk 101 Lulu and B57 depth charge weapons to airbases across Europe for use by US and allied maritime patrol aircraft and anti-submarine helicopters. The Mk 101 Lulu had a yield or explosive power equivalent to 11 kilotons of TNT, so was smaller than the weapons dropped on Hiroshima and Nagasaki. The B57 had five different variants with yields between five and 20 kilotons. The weapons were intended to detonate hundreds of feet underwater to kill submarines by vaporising them in the fire ball or crushing their hulls with a pressure wave.

The idea was to use these in situations where there was not time to hunt down and kill Soviet submarines with conventional weapons, such as when a ballistic missile boat was preparing to fire its weapons or when a group of submarines were gathering to stage a wolf-pack style attack on an allied naval task force.

The US Navy's Atlantic Command oversaw the plan and established two storage sites for the weapons in Britain during 1968. The sites were at RAF

St Mawgan in Cornwall and RAF Machrihanish on the Mull of Kintyre. US Marines guarded the specially built nuclear weapon bunkers and held the depth charges ready for US Navy, British and Dutch maritime patrol aircraft, or helicopters to collect in time of conflict. The two British bases were the main nuclear depth charge storage sites for the North Atlantic region, because Iceland, Norway and Denmark refused to allow US nuclear weapons to be stored at their air bases.

Britain had its own version, the WE177, which were embarked on larger warships and aircraft carriers for employment by Royal Navy helicopters. They were also stored at RAF Kinloss in Scotland for use by RAF maritime patrol aircraft.

As with all nuclear weapon concepts of the Cold War era, the idea of using nuclear depth charges sounded better on paper than it would have worked out in practice. During NATO tactical evaluation drills, the procedures for authorising and authenticating the order for the release of tactical nuclear weapons proved to be highly bureaucratic and time consuming. In these exercises, getting simulated clearances for US depth charges to be released for use by allied aircraft took several hours as all military commanders involved tried to get approval from their respective governments.

Many of the participants in these exercises were left wondering what would happen in a real war, when the Soviets would have been shooting back and trying to interrupt allied radio communications. Thankfully, this was one anti-submarine tactic that they never had to try out for real.

LEFT: A WE177 training nuclear bomb preserved at the Explosion Museum of Naval Firepower in Gosport. The British-designed and made nuclear bomb and depth charge was in use with the Royal Navy and Royal Air Force from 1966 to 1998. (THE WUB)

Nimrod

The Mighty Hunter

The jet powered Hawker Siddeley Nimrod is sometimes called the best anti-submarine aircraft ever to enter Royal Air Force service.

It began life in 1964 with the issuing of Air Staff Requirement 381 for a new maritime patrol aircraft to replace the Avro Shackleton, which was suffering from airframe fatigue issues. The new aircraft needed to enter service by the end of the decade.

The British Ministry of Defence considered several designs for the new aircraft. America offered the Lockheed P-3 Orion, which was just entering service, and the French pitched the Breguet Br.1150 Atlantic. Several British aviation companies also proposed solutions, based on converted airliners, including the BAC One Eleven, the Vickers VC-10, Hawker Siddeley Trident and the de Havilland Comet. In less than a year, the Hawker Siddeley company won the contract to build the aircraft, which was soon named the Nimrod, after the mighty hunter in Greek mythology.

Hawker Siddeley now owned the de Havilland brand and proposed converting their Comet 4 airliner into the Nimrod at its Woodford site in Cheshire, where the former Avro company had built the famous

Lancaster bomber and then the Shackleton.

The Nimrod kept the Comet's distinctive wing design with four Rolls-Royce Spey engines embedded into its wing-roots. Major conversion work included the addition of a new pressurised 'double-bubble' fuselage cabin above the wings. This gave the aircraft its unique front aspect, with the top of the fuselage looking bigger than the lower fuselage. The lower

LEFT: The Nimrod's pressurised 'double-bubble' cabin made the aircraft instantly recognisable and differentiated the maritime patrol aircraft from the Comet airliner. (BAE SYTEMS)

fuselage was modified to incorporate a bomb bay for depth charges and torpedoes. A surface surveillance radar was mounted in the nose and a magnetic anomaly boom was fitted behind the tail.

As the world's first ever jet powered maritime patrol aircraft, the Nimrod had the ability to rapidly transit to patrol areas, saving valuable time and fuel. Once on station, the Nimrod could close down two engines to save fuel and still be able to rapidly react to sensor contacts. The aircraft was also highly manoeuvrable at low level so could still rapidly execute dive bombing attacks on any submarines found on the surface.

The Nimrod was also the first British – and second in the world - maritime patrol aircraft to be fitted with a computerised acoustic system. Just like the Lockheed P-3 Orion, which featured a similar system, the Nimrod's mission crew were able to receive track information from sonobuoys and then use it to generate tactical maps showing the location of target submarines on computer screens. This replaced the analogue acoustic systems used in the old Shackletons, which crews had to manually monitor. The track information from these systems had to be drawn on paper charts to calculate the position of submarines which was a labour intensive and very slow process.

Hawker Siddeley's new aircraft flew for the first time in May 1967 and the first production aircraft was handed over to the RAF in October 1969. This allowed them to begin to convert Shackleton crews to fly the new aircraft and the following year the first Nimrod MR1s began flying operational missions around the North Atlantic from RAF Kinloss in Scotland.

When allied maritime patrol crews saw the Nimrod for the first time, they expressed admiration for the sleek looking jet aircraft that had far better underwater sensors than anything they flew. RAF Nimrod crews won the annual Fincastle Competition of anti-submarine skills six times between 1970 and 1977. This pitted maritime patrol crews from Australia, Britain, Canada, and New Zealand against each other in tactical drills involving a live submarine. The performance of the Nimrod in the Fincastle and in operational tasking to track »

BELOW: The Nimrod's cockpit was from its time and had very few modern electronics. (TIM RIPLEY)

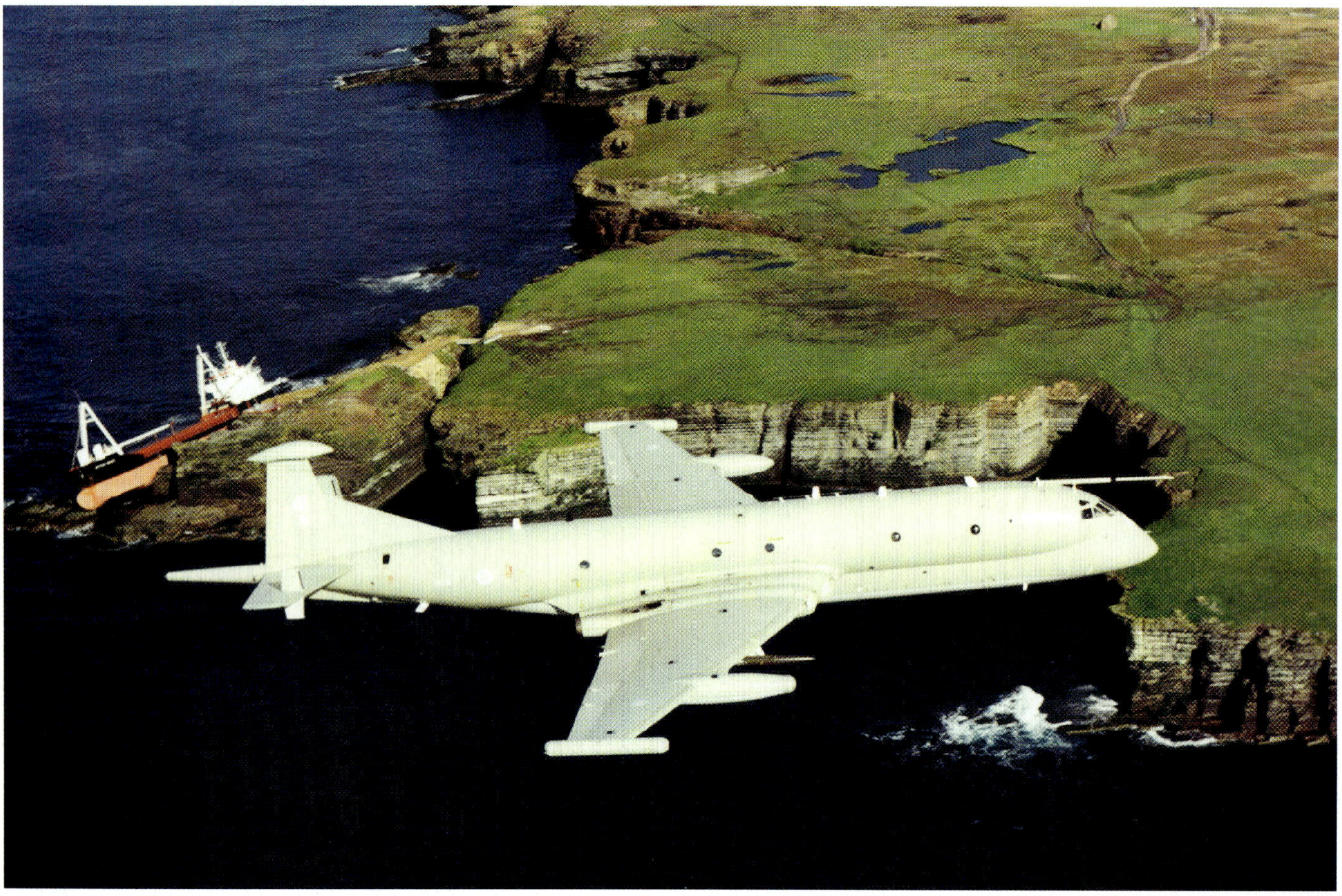

ABOVE: The Nimrod MR2 variant sported Orange Crop electronic support system pods on its wing tips and strakes on its horizontal tail stabiliser, which were fitted to counteract the aerodynamic effects of the installation of an air-to-air refuelling probe after the 1982 Falklands conflict. (BAE SYTEMS)

Soviet submarines in the North Atlantic enhanced the reputation of the RAF maritime patrol force across NATO and further afield, helping to establish its position as a leading player in the allied effort to counter the Soviet underwater threat.

NIMROD MR.2
Crew: 13
Capacity: 13,500lb (6,123kg)
Length: 126ft 9in (38.63m)
Wingspan: 114ft 10in (35m)
Max take-off weight: 192,000lb (87,090kg)
Powerplant: Four × Rolls-Royce Spey turbofan engines
Cruise speed: 426kts (490mph, 789kph)
Range: 4,500 to 5,000nm (8,300–9,200km)
Armament:
Air-to-air missile: Two × AIM-9 Sidewinder
Air-to-surface missile: AGM-84 Harpoon
Nuclear Weapons: Two × US-owned B57 depth bombs, WE.177A depth charges
Air-dropped Mk.46, Sting Ray torpedoes

Operational Squadrons

By 1971 the RAF had five operational squadrons which were based at RAF Kinloss, RAF St Mawgan in Cornwall, and RAF Luqa on Malta in the Mediterranean. A total of 46 maritime patrol variants of the Nimrod were built at Woodford.

The pace of Soviet submarine development meant that even before the last Nimrod MR1s were delivered work had begun to upgrade the aircraft, to MR2 standard. The nose mounted surface surveillance radar was replaced with the Searchwater radar, which could detect submarine periscopes and snorkels at long ranges. Major improvements were made to the acoustic system to increase the number of sonobuoys the

RIGHT: A Nimrod MR2 tactical controller and navigator at work in the aircraft's mission area. (TIM RIPLEY)

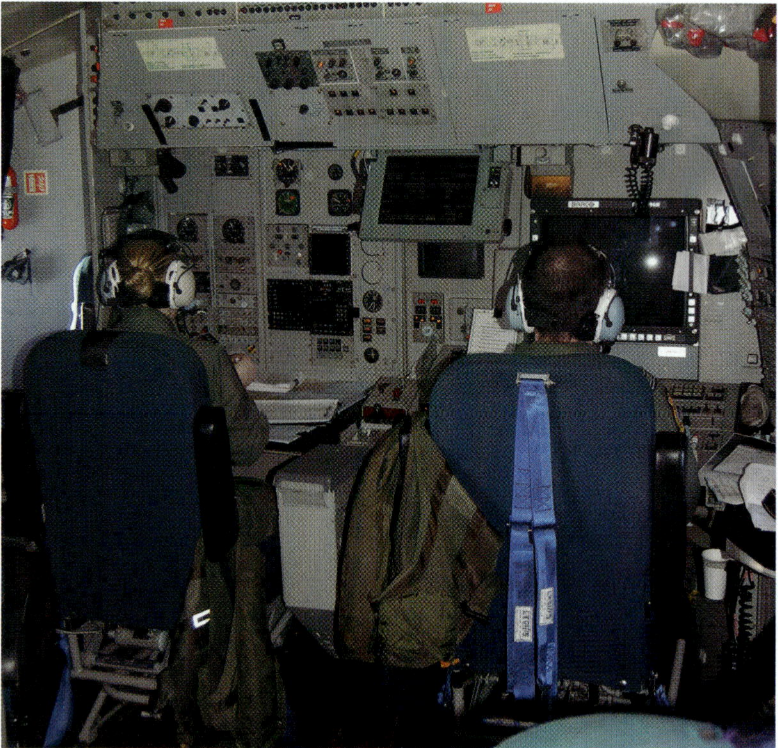

aircraft could control. It was also to be armed with the British-made Stingray homing torpedo. Beginning in 1975, 35 MR1 aircraft were converted to the new standard.

In 1982, Nimrod MR2s were dispatched to the South Atlantic to support the British naval task force that was sent to recapture the Falkland Islands. To enable them to reach the Falklands, a number of Nimrods were converted to allow them to carry out air-to-air refuelling. Sidewinder air-to-air missiles were also fitted to provide protection from Argentine fighter jets. The primary role of the Nimrods in the Falklands was to detect the Argentine surface fleet, rather than hunt hostile submarines.

The end of the Cold War in 1990, saw the RAF Nimrod fleet being reduced and the remaining aircraft were concentrated at RAF Kinloss. With no submarines left to hunt, the remaining Nimrods were re-tasked to monitor merchant shipping trying to breach United Nation trade sanctions against Iraq and Serbia. After the 9/11 attacks on New York, the Nimrod picked up a new role providing an 'eye in the sky' for special forces teams operating in Afghanistan and Iraq, using new electro-optical video cameras.

In 1996 a programme was launched to replace the MR2 with an improved version, the MRA4. This had better sensors, new engines, new wings, and a refurbished fuselage. The first of the new aircraft were supposed to

enter service in 2003 but the project suffered major technical problems and cost overruns which delayed work for seven years.

These problems meant the RAF had to run the old MR2s beyond their planned retirement date and corners were cut in maintenance of the aircraft. After an MR2 was lost over Afghanistan in 2006, as a result of a fuel leak in the air-to-air refuelling systems, an official inquiry blamed the RAF for neglecting the airworthiness of the Nimrod fleet.

After being modified, the MR2 fleet returned to flight status but the aircraft were withdrawn from service in March 2010 as part of a cost cutting exercise. The RAF was banking on the arrival of the first of the new MRA4s later in the year to fill its maritime patrol gap. However, the October 2010 defence review cancelled the order and three months later the nine almost complete MRA4 aircraft were broken up for scrap at BAE Systems Woodford plant. It was a sad end to the mighty hunter's 40 year career.

ABOVE: The Nimrod MRA4 was the proposed replacement for the MR2 variant but it was scrapped in 2010 before even entering RAF service after technical problems led to cost overruns and delays. (BAE SYTEMS)

BELOW: A pair of Nimrod MR2s overly fly RAF Kinloss, which was home to the type from 1970 until its retirement in March 2010. (BAE SYTEMS)

The Falklands 1982

Anti-Submarine Action

During the 46 years of the Cold War standoff between the Soviet Union and the United States, neither side's navies fired a shot in anger against their adversary. Despite the huge amounts spent on submarine and underwater technology, they were never put the ultimate test in live combat.

The only shooting war of the Cold War era involving submarines took place during the brief conflict in the South Atlantic between Britain and Argentina in 1982. Both sides had modern navies and employed their anti-submarine forces against their enemy's submarines.

The British Royal Navy had the edge. It sent three nuclear-powered attack submarines to the South Atlantic and the British naval task force was protected by modern anti-submarine helicopters.

Argentina had only two operational conventionally powered submarines, a 1950s vintage ex-US Guppy-class boat and a recently delivered German-made Type 209. Its anti-submarine technology was mainly American, which dated from the 1950s or 1960s. The Argentine navy's main maritime patrol aircraft were Lockheed P-2 Neptunes and Grumman S-2 Trackers. Most Argentine warships had depth charges but no homing torpedoes. However, the Argentines had the

home advantage and only had to inflict a few losses on the British to derail their invasion to re-capture the disputed Falkland Islands.

The British scored an early success when Royal Navy helicopters caught

the US-supplied ARA *Sante Fe* on the surface on April 25, as she was leaving harbour on South Georgia and attacked her with missiles and depth charges. She was captured largely intact when British Royal Marines seized the island.

British signals intelligence was monitoring Argentine naval communications, and this gave the Royal Navy advance warning of submarine attacks. On May 1, British aircraft attacked Port Stanley airport on the Falklands and Royal Navy warships closed to the islands to bombard coastal defences. Signals intelligence indicated the Argentine's other operational submarine, ARA *San Luis*, was north of Port Stanley preparing to engage the British warships. HMS *Yarmouth* and HMS *Brilliant* were dispatched to hunt it down and three Westland Sea King HAS5 helicopters of 826 Naval Air Squadron were sent to help the search. The Sea Kings used their dipping sonars and dropped sonobuoys, while the frigates used their hull-mounted sonars during a 20-hour long search. The Sea

Kings were refuelled in the air via hoses from the frigates and several contacts were made, leading to six Mark 11 depth charges and two Mk 46 homing torpedoes being dropped by the Sea Kings. The captain of the ARA *San Luis* later reported that he had made an abortive attack on the warships with two wire guided torpedoes but they both malfunctioned. So, he grounded his boat on the seabed to wait out the British.

The Royal Navy's HMS *Conqueror* sank the Argentine cruiser ARA General Belgrano on May 2, 1982, but she managed to easily escape pursuing warships and Argentine Neptunes by diving deep and accelerating away from the engagement zone.

Eight days later the ARA *San Luis* tried to attack again, firing a torpedo at HMS *Alacrity* as she was transiting out of Falklands Sound. The weapon was later found to have been spoofed by the frigate's Type 183 towed decoy.

Neither British nor Argentine anti-submarine forces were able to successfully find and engage enemy submarines. In the open sea, modern attack submarines - both conventional and nuclear-powered - seemed to have the edge.

ABOVE: Argentina had two German-made Submarine Type 209-class diesel powered submarine in 1982 but only one, the ARA *San Luis*, was fit to go to sea. (MARTIN OTERO)

LEFT: P-2 Neptunes were the Argentine naval aviation's only shore based anti-submarine aircraft and they made several missions, without success, to hunt for British nuclear-powered attack submarines. (ARGENTINE NAVY)

Russia's Submarines

The New Threat

The formal demise of the Soviet Union in December 1991 led to the formation of the Russian Federation. This was followed by the formal transformation of the Soviet Navy into the Russian Navy in January 1992.

Russia's economy went into free-fall after the collapse of communism and the new government in the Kremlin ordered huge cuts in military spending. The Russian navy's submarine force was dramatically reduced. Significant manpower cuts and base closures followed. A major preoccupation became the dismantling of redundant Soviet

submarines and their surplus nuclear reactor cores.

The remnants of the Russian submarine fleet were concentrated in the Northern Fleet at bases on the Kola Peninsula, around the Arctic city of Murmansk. At its height in the mid-1980s the Northern Fleet had 176 submarines in service, including 45 SSBNs, 68 (SSN) and cruise missile firing nuclear powered submarines (SSGNs), and 63 conventional attack submarines (SSKs). By 2018, the Northern Fleet had been reduced to just 32 frontline submarines. The reliance on conscript sailors was reduced with them being allocated to shore roles or work on surface war ships, making the submarine force the domain of professional or contract sailors.

But many things remained the same. The Northern Fleet remained in the forefront of Russian nuclear submarine development, with the organisation being responsible for the entry to service of new classes of boats, new weapons, or sensor systems. Nuclear deterrent submarine operations remained centred on the Northern Fleet »

RIGHT: The 1990s saw a mass scrapping of redundant Soviet nuclear submarines and western countries helped Russia dispose of their old nuclear reactors. (@ARTJOMH)

BELOW: Gadzhiyevo is home to the 31st Submarine Division, which controls all the Northern Fleet's SSBNs, and the Akula-class attack boats of the 24th Submarine Division. (MAXAR TECHNOLOGIES)

PACIFIC FLEET

The remainder of Russia's nuclear submarine fleet is based in the Far East at Vilyuchinsk. The Pacific Fleet's older submarines are being retired or upgraded. These include three Oscar IIs and one Akula attack submarine, as well as one old Delta III and two new Borei SSBNs.

LEFT: The Project 941 Akula (shark) SSBN is the 'classic' Cold War submarine made famous in the Hollywood movie, *The Hunt for Red October*, and was dubbed Typhoon by NATO. Only one of these giant SSBNs, the *Dmitriy Donskoy* (TK-208), now remains in service and it is used for testing and trials work linked to the troubled Bulava ballistic missile. The entry to service of this missile in 2018 suggested that the final Typhoon could be soon destined for scrap. Its Russian name Akula is rather confusing because NATO used the name to describe a different class of attack submarines. (@REJERCITOS)

BELOW: The Project 9551 Borei (NATO: Dolgoruky) is the new generation of Russian SSBN. The first of the class entered service with the Northern Fleet in 2013. This process was considerably delayed by technical issues with the Bulava ballistic missiles which were not fully resolved until 2018. An improved variant, the Project 9552 Borei A, which incorporates changes to its internal design, finally entered Northern Fleet service in May 2020. (RUSSIAN NAVY)

ABOVE: Project 667DRM Delfin (NATO: Delta IV) is a Soviet-era submarine that now bears the brunt of nuclear deterrent patrol duty. All six remaining Delta IV boats were built during the 1980s and early 1990s. They have all been refurbished since 2010 and this suggests they could be in service until well into the 2020s. (@CAPTNAVY)

RIGHT: Project 945A Kondor (NATO: Sierra II) Soviet-era SSNs were built in the late 1980s and early 1990s. They have Titanium hulls and were considered the quietest Soviet-era boats. They are still considered useful by the Russian Navy. Two of the boats have been overhauled over the past decade but decisions to overhaul the remaining two boats have still not been made. (RUSSIAN NAVY)

RIGHT: The Project 671RTM/RTMK Shchuka or Pike (NATO: Victor-III) submarines were the workhorses of the Soviet attack submarine fleet in the 1980s but only three remain in service. These all entered service between 1990 and 1992, so they are some of the newest boats in the Northern Fleet. One has been recently overhauled and modernised. It is unclear if the remaining two will modernised. (US DOD)

and the Barents Sea. The Russian Northern Fleet, its subordinate units and vessels retained many of the traditions and honours of their Soviet predecessors. For example, it still retained the formal Red Banner honour bestowed on its Soviet predecessor in 1965.

The nadir of the post-Soviet Northern Fleet was the sinking of the submarine RFS *Kursk* in 2000 with the loss of 118 sailors. The incident was a major embarrassment for the Russian Navy and the newly appointed Russian President Vladimir Putin which led to a significant boost in the funding to the Russian Navy

BELOW: The Project 949A Antey (NATO: Oscar II) are the last of the Soviet-era SSGNs and boast a huge weapon load, including 24 P-700 Granit (SS-N-19) nuclear or conventionally armed cruise missiles and 24 torpedoes. One of the Northern Fleet's three submarines has been overhauled and work is underway on the second of the class. It has been suggested that these submarines will eventually be fitted with the Kalibr 1,500km-range precision-guided, conventionally armed cruise missile. This weapon is the Russian equivalent of the US Tomahawk land-attack missile and its employment in Syria in 2015 and Ukraine from 2023 transformed the strike capabilities of the Russian Navy. The ill-fated *Kursk* was an Oscar-II. (MOD/CROWN COPYRIGHT)

BLACK SEA FLEET AND MEDITERRANEAN FLOTILLA

The Black Sea Fleet took the first six of the Improved Kilo-class conventional submarines into service. Up until 2022, these submarines routinely operated in the Mediterranean and they fired Kalibr cruise missiles at targets in Syria. Since the start of the war with Ukraine in February 2022, the fleet's submarines have fired hundreds of cruise missiles at Ukraine. One Kilo-class submarine was destroyed in a Ukraine missile strike on Sevastopol harbour in 2023.

and its submarine arm. These measures were part of a programme of modernisation across the Russian armed forces aimed at improving its readiness, capabilities, and effectiveness to enable them to enhance Russia's geo-political position.

The Northern Fleet currently boasts a mixed flotilla of submarine types, which are a mix of ex-Soviet and new build vessels. There is a small force of conventional attack submarines based around the Project 877-class (NATO: Kilo) and the new Project 677 or Lada-class (NATO: St Petersburg). Its five Kilos are some of the oldest Kilo-class submarines still in service and are not fitted with Kalibr cruise missiles. Only the Improved Kilo or Project 636.3 boats have this weapon, but none are in service with the Northern Fleet. Two Northern Fleet Kilos are in the process of being scrapped.

The days of the Cold War, when the Northern Fleet could field 176 submarines, including 68 attack boats, and threaten to overwhelm NATO navies in the North Atlantic are very much in the past.

ABOVE: The Project 885 Yasen or Ash Tree and Yasen-M (NATO: Yasen) are the newest - and most expensive - attack boats in Russian Navy service. The cost and complexity of the project has meant it took five years from the first boat entering service in 2013 to the second boat beginning sea trials in September 2018. Its formal entry into service was delayed by technical problems in the SEVMASH shipyard and it did not enter service until May 2021. As standard, they are fitted to fire Kalibr cruise missiles. The next four submarines to be built are destined for the Northern Fleet but it is unclear which fleets will operate the next six submarines on order. The second boat is of the enhanced Yasen-M configuration. (@RUSSIANSUB)

Pacific Challenge

Chinese Submarines in the 21st Century

In the Pacific region, the Chinese navy offers a very different threat in terms of scale and technology. According to the US intelligence estimates, in 2023 China spent $700bn on defence, growing its defence budget for the 28th consecutive year. This more than four times that of Russia.

Beijing naval forces are just on a very different scale to those of Russia and dwarf the size of other navies in the Pacific region. The Chinese People's Liberation Army Navy's (PLAN) surface fleet is enormous, with 51 destroyers, 49 frigates, 70 corvettes and 109 missile boats. They are backed up by 79 submarines, including at least nine nuclear-powered attack boats and seven ballistic missile firing boats. More nuclear-powered submarines are under construction.

Work on nuclear-powered submarines began in 1958 when the Central Military Commission gave approval to start the Type 091 submarine project. The leader of communist China, Mao Zedong declared that China would build nuclear attack submarines "even if it took ten thousand years." It didn't take the nation 10,000 years but it was 1974 before the first submarine in the class, PLANS *Changzheng 1* (Long March 1), was launched.

The Type 091 was China's first-generation nuclear-powered attack submarine. Six boats of the class were built and two have since been retired as more modern Type 093 submarines came on line in 2006.

Two of these boats were built before a new sub-class, the Type 093A, arrived. The first boat of this class was laid down in 2009 and was commissioned in 2015. Four of these new vessels were built and they had a greater length and a hump behind the sail.

Development of a new variant, Type 093B, armed with surface/land-attack missiles is under way and

two submarines were laid down in 2022 and 2023.

Building on its experience with attack submarines, the PLAN began work on a new class of ballistic missile firing nuclear-powered submarines in 1978. The sole Type 092 entered service in 1983. It bore many similarities in layout to the Russian Yankee and Delta-class of missile boats but was not a success, and no more missile boats were laid down for the remainder of the century.

Work on the successor class, the Type 094, began in 2001 when the first boat was laid down. The first Type 094 submarine entered service in 2007 and over the following 14 years five more boats were built.

China's naval strategy is an evolution of Russia's Anti-Access/Area Denial (or A2/AD) concept which is aimed at making it very difficult for the US and other Western navies to operate close its coast. At the same time, China's growing blue water navy gives it the capability to challenge the US and its allies in their home waters.

The summer of 2022 saw the Chinese put on a show of naval power around the disputed island of Taiwan, with missile tests and air exercises taking place. They appeared to be a rehearsal for an expanded Chinese operation to blockade Taiwan and prevent the US Navy from intervening to stop an amphibious landing.

Nuclear submarine force plays an import role in the PLAN's plans to confront US naval power in the South China Sea and in the wider Pacific region. Its growing capabilities are of serious concern to the leadership of the US Navy and its regional allies.

ABOVE: Thirteen Type 039, or Song-class, conventionally-powered attack submarines are currently operated by the **PLAN.** (STEKUEBE)

BELOW: Six Type 094, or Jin-class, ballistic missile firing nuclear-powered submarines are currently in PLAN service and two more are reported to be being built. (US NAVY OFFICE OF LEGISLATIVE AFFAIRS)

From the Hermit Kingdom

North Korea's Submarine

It is notoriously difficult to assess the military capacity of North Korea, or as it calls itself, the Democratic People's Republic of Korea (DPRK). The highly secretive state refuses to let foreign observers access its armed forces or defence industries.

In the decades after the 1950-53 Korean war, the DPRK relied on Chinese and Soviet military aid. During this period, its navy received four former Soviet Whiskey-class submarines, 22 Chinese Romeo-class submarines, and 20 DPRK-built Romeo-class submarines, known as the Type 033. It is unclear how many of these vintage submarines remain in service today, but they are far less capable than modern attack submarines.

As the Cold War cooled in the late 1980s, Beijing and Moscow cut their arms supplies and the North Koreans had to build up their own defence industry.

In 1991 the first of 41 Sang-O class of coastal submarines entered service. They are larger than a midget submarine, but smaller than the old Romeo and Whiskey-class vessels. They are equipped with four torpedo tubes and 16 mines, but some are unarmed and are used to carry North Korean commandos.

Construction of a more modern class of submarine, the Snipo, began in 2014 and a new variant was launched in 2023 which appeared to have ballistic missile tubes installed behind its sail. Known as the Snipo-C, the new submarines are part of North Korea's build up of missile forces to threaten South Korea, Japan, and the United States.

The first of class was launched on September 6, 2023, as *Hero Kim Kun Ok* and christened and commissioned on the following day. Both events were attended by North Korean leader, Kim Jong-un, and the submarine was promoted by North Korean media as the "first of its kind" designed for "core underwater offensive means".

Iran's Subs

Gulf Naval Power

Since the Iranian revolution of 1979, the Middle Eastern country has been developing its navy to protect its oil exports and confront the US naval presence in the Arabian Gulf region.

After Iranian naval vessels were hit by US airstrikes in confrontations during the Iran-Iraq war in the 1980s, the Iranians launched a plan to rebuild their naval power. In 1988 Tehran place an order for three Kilo-class conventionally-powered submarines with a shipyard in the then Leningrad, which was part of the Soviet Union. The submarines were delivered from the newly established Russia in 1991 and 1993. They were the first submarines ever to see service in the Iranian navy and in a Gulf region navy.

These submarines remain in service with the Iranian navy, and they have given it invaluable experience in underwater warfare.

This century, the Iranian navy launched their first home-built submarines and in 2013 launched the first Fateh-class coastal submarine. To date only one, the INS *Fateh* has been built. According to Iranian statements, she is equipped with, surface-to-surface guided missiles and torpedoes.

Iran has shown considerable interest in acquiring midget submarines for use in sabotage attacks. It reportedly bought midget submarines from North Korea in the 1990s.

The existence of the Ghadir-class of midget submarines emerged early this century and up to 21 have been built in an Iranian shipyard over the past two decades.

Existence of a Nahang-class midget submarine emerged in 2006 but only one is believed to have been constructed. In 2017, the US Office of Naval Intelligence reported that Iran purchased at least one Yono-class submarine from North Korea in that year.

ABOVE: Three Kilo-class diesel submarines were purchased from the Soviet Union in 1988 and they were towed to Iran in the early 1990s to allow crew training to begin. (US DOD)

LEFT: One Fateh-class semi-heavy submarine is currently in service with the Islamic Republic of Iran Navy and three more are being built. (HOSSEIN ZOHREVAD)

A New Cold War

A New Response

RIGHT: The Norwegian frigate **HNLMS** *Van Amstel* trains with the Dutch submarine **HNLMS** *Zeeleeuw*. (MOD/CROWN COPYRIGHT)

Over the two decades that followed the end of the Cold War, the huge global surveillance apparatus set up to monitor the Soviet navy was progressively dismantled. With the threat seemingly gone, NATO armed forces switched their focus to peacekeeping and counter-terrorist missions in the Balkans, Africa, Middle East, and Afghanistan. The US SOSUS nets were largely dismantled, and the RAF took a maritime patrol 'holiday' for a decade when it scrapped its Nimrods in 2010. Many other NATO nations also slimmed down their maritime patrol aircraft fleets. The Netherlands got out of the maritime patrol business for good, selling off its P-3P aircraft to Germany.

This all changed in February 2014 when Russian troops seized control of the Crimea Peninsula. Moscow was now directly threatening western interests. At the same time, in the Pacific, Chinese naval forces had been progressively building their strength, including expanding their nuclear-powered submarine fleet. Naval confrontations with Russia and China were now real, not something in the imagination of academic think tanks.

A decade ago, the US Navy began recapitalising its maritime patrol aircraft fleet and contracted Boeing

BELOW: A US Navy P-8A Poseidon anti-submarine warfare patrol aircraft, assigned to Patrol Squadron VP 46, left, sits on the flight-line next to its British counterpart at RAF Lossiemouth. Forward deployed Poseidons operate under the control of to the US 6th Fleet's Task Force 67, which is responsible for tactical control of deployed maritime patrol and reconnaissance squadrons throughout Europe and Africa. (US NAVY)

to begin serial production of its P-8 Poseidon. The RAF, Norway, Germany, and Canada have since followed and ordered the new aircraft. At nearly $200m each, even the US Navy has not managed to replace its old P-3 fleet with P-8s on a one-for-one basis, with only 128 of the new aircraft on order compared to more than 600 P-3s that were built for the service. This means that there is little prospect of replicating a Cold War-era level of maritime patrol aircraft activity in the NATO area or the Western Pacific. However, the new generation of maritime patrol aircraft now in production are more sophisticated and capable thanks to improvements in their sensors and data analysis capabilities.

Modern maritime patrol aircraft now have far more effective sonobuoys than their Cold War era counterparts thanks to advances in computer technology and data links used in the devices. These new sonobuoys have longer sensor and data transmission ranges. They are also multi-role so a sonobuoy field dropped by a P-8 can be controlled or monitored by an anti-submarine helicopter operating from a warship, enabling multiple platforms to join together in integrated operations against specific submarines. These developments all mean fewer aircraft and helicopters can monitor greater areas of ocean than their Cold War counter-parts.

While the technological improvements compensate for some of the reduction in numbers, other operators are looking to fill gaps with other capabilities. The UK, for example, is proposing to augment its P-8 by using its soon to be delivered General Atomics Protector unmanned aerial vehicles in a maritime surveillance role. As well as flying them for overwater surveillance missions around the UK coast and further out into the North Atlantic from their home base at RAF Waddington in Lincolnshire, the RAF is giving serious consideration

to equipping its Protectors with dispensers to drop sonobuoys. Then the sonobuoy fields could be controlled remotely, via the Protector, or taken over by anti-submarine helicopters and P-8s. Other nations are looking to use UAVs in the anti-submarine role, including small drones armed with torpedoes that are intended to be launched from frigates.

Aerial surveillance of the world's oceans – both above and below the waves – is still a key military requirement. Some surveillance burden can be taken by satellites or unmanned drones but as yet, the manned maritime patrol aircraft remain highly useful, particularly when it comes to the final stages of hunting down and possibly destroying hostile submarines. Any future battle of the Atlantic will be very different from the 1943 iteration, but maritime airpower will still be decisive.

Underwater Detection

SOSUS for the 21st century

RIGHT: The ocean surveillance ship USNS *Able* of the US Military Sealift Command during acceptance sea trials in March, 1992. She was eventually converted to operate the SURTASS Low Frequency Active Sonar System to carry out underwater surveillance at an oceanic scale. (US NAVY)

I n the 21st century a very different surveillance challenge faces US and NATO naval commanders. Just like in the Cold War, it is now relatively easy to use satellite surveillance to watch for when Russian submarines and warships put to sea from their bases near Murmansk on the Kola Peninsula, or in the Baltic Sea. A new generation of heat detecting, and radar-based earth observation satellites mean that Russian naval bases can now be monitored continuously in bad weather. This technology is now widely available at low cost and even private sector satellite providers put infra-red and radar imagery on the open market.

This technology also allows surface vessels to be monitored when they are at sea, and it has revolutionised naval warfare. It is now almost impossible for a major warship to 'disappear' from view for any length of time, even in the middle of an ocean. This used to be the bread and butter of NATO maritime patrol aircraft units but the real-time tracking of Russian surface vessels far out in the North Atlantic can now largely be left to satellite surveillance.

When Russian vessels start to head close to the territorial waters of NATO nations then maritime patrol aircraft and surface warships are sent to shadow them to make sure they follow the 'laws of the sea' concerning peaceful passage through allied waters.

EARS UNDER THE SEA

The US Military Sea Lift Command operates a fleet of five specialist ships that are equipped to tow Deployable Surveillance Systems (DSS) or sonar arrays.

BELOW: In March 2009 Chinese trawlers forced ocean surveillance ship USNS *Impeccable* to conduct an emergency 'all stop' in order to avoid collision in international waters in the South China Sea about 75 miles south of Hainan Island. (US NAVY)

The situation is very different for submarines. The days of fixed SOSUS nets are gone and the US Navy is now in the process of expanding a modern successor system. Its new plans call for oceanic-level surveillance to be carried by a mix of sensors on allied warships, maritime patrol aircraft, and submarines, augmented by data from the remaining fixed sonar arrays and specialist towed arrays. Acoustic data is transmitted in real time back to two control hubs where giant super computers then merge all this data and create undersea charts showing the position of friendly and hostile submarines.

The US Navy's Theater Undersea Surveillance Command Atlantic (TUSC LANT) hub is at Dam Neck in Virginia and Theater Undersea Surveillance Command Pacific (TUSC PAC) is at Oak Harbor in Washington. The US Navy says TUSC LANT: "conducts continuous maritime surveillance for undersea domain awareness, which provides timely and accurate acoustic intelligence reporting and cueing to theater undersea warfare commanders using fixed, mobile, and deployable assets across the world in support of homeland defense and national security 24/7/365."

According to the US Navy: "TUSC LANT has become the premier undersea surveillance site, conducting operations throughout the Atlantic Ocean, Mediterranean and Norwegian Seas. TUSC LANT is manned at 368 personnel consisting of 15 US officers, three United Kingdom officers, one Canadian officer, seven civilians, 285 US sailors, and 56 UK sailors and airmen. In May 2009, TUSC LANT officially became a Joint Combined Command welcoming a United Kingdom Detachment comprised of both Royal Navy and Royal Air Force personnel and an increased area of responsibility. TUSC LANT proudly hosts the largest contingent of United Kingdom personnel in the United States."

With this god's eye view of the undersea environment, US and allied commanders can task maritime patrol aircraft, anti-submarine helicopters, and other assets to closely mark any suspicious submarines that venture close to allied territorial waters or vulnerable underwater infra-structure, such as trans-Atlantic internet cables or gas pipelines.

US MILITARY SEA LIFT COMMAND OCEAN SURVEILLANCE SHIPS	
Victorious-Class	
USNS *Victorious*	(T-AGOS-19)
USNS *Able*	(T-AGOS-20)
USNS *Effective*	(T-AGOS-21)
USNS *Loyal*	(T-AGOS-22)
Impeccable-class	
USNS *Impeccable*	(T-AGOS-23)

Boeing's P-8A Poseidon

The New Generation

After nearly 60 years of frontline service the US Navy retired its last Lockheed P-3C Orion maritime patrol aircraft from frontline service in May 2020. The milestone marked the point that the stalwart Orion finally passed the baton to the Boeing P-8A Poseidon, the US Navy's next generation submarine hunting aircraft.

The Orion and Poseidon are very different, and the new aircraft is designed to hunt and kill submarines in a very new way.

During 1989, the US made its first bid to replace the Orion when it awarded Lockheed a contract to develop the P-7A LRAACA, or

Long-Range Air ASW-Capable Aircraft. The timing could not have been worse. In November 1989, the Berlin Wall was pulled down, effectively ending the Cold War. The following year the LRAACA project was cancelled as part of a massive cutback in defence spending ordered by the Pentagon.

It took another decade for the US Navy to find the money to restart the programme after reports emerged that the P-3 fleet was affected by fatigue and erosion problems. In 2000 a competition was launched for a replacement, Lockheed Martin proposed a rebuilt P-3, dubbed Orion 21, and Boeing offered a modified 737 airliner. The British company

US NAVY P-8A SQUADRONS, JANUARY 2024

Unit/Base	Role	Nicknames	Location
US Naval Air Forces Pacific			
Patrol and Reconnaissance Wing 10			Naval Air Station Whidbey Island, Washington
VP-1	Maritime Patrol/Anti-Submarine Warfare	Screaming Eagles	Naval Air Station Whidbey Island, Washington
VP-4	Maritime Patrol/Anti-Submarine Warfare	Skinny Dragons	Naval Air Station Whidbey Island, Washington
VP-9	Maritime Patrol/Anti-Submarine Warfare	Golden Eagles	Naval Air Station Whidbey Island, Washington
VP-40	Maritime Patrol/Anti-Submarine Warfare	Fighting Marlins	Naval Air Station Whidbey Island, Washington
VP-46	Maritime Patrol/Anti-Submarine Warfare	Grey Knights	Naval Air Station Whidbey Island, Washington
VP-47	Maritime Patrol/Anti-Submarine Warfare	Golden Swordsmen	Naval Air Station Whidbey Island, Washington
VP-69 (Naval Air Reserve)	Maritime Patrol/Anti-Submarine Warfare	Totems	Naval Air Station Whidbey Island, Washington
US Naval Air Forces Atlantic			
VX-1	Anti-Submarine Warfare Test & Evaluation	Pioneers	Naval Air Station Patuxent River, Maryland
Patrol and Reconnaissance Wing 11			Naval Air Station Jacksonville, Florida
VPU-2	Signals/Communications Intelligence	Wizards	Naval Air Station Jacksonville, Florida
VP-5	Maritime Patrol/Anti-Submarine Warfare	Mad Foxes	Naval Air Station Jacksonville, Florida
VP-8	Maritime Patrol/Anti-Submarine Warfare	Tigers	Naval Air Station Jacksonville, Florida
VP-10	Maritime Patrol/Anti-Submarine Warfare	Red Lancers	Naval Air Station Jacksonville, Florida
VP-16	Maritime Patrol/Anti-Submarine Warfare	War Eagles	Naval Air Station Jacksonville, Florida
VP-26	Maritime Patrol/Anti-Submarine Warfare	Tridents	Naval Air Station Jacksonville, Florida
VP-30	Fleet Replacement/Crew Conversion	Pro's Nest	Naval Air Station Jacksonville, Florida
VP-45	Maritime Patrol/Anti-Submarine Warfare	Pelicans	Naval Air Station Jacksonville, Florida
VP-62 (Naval Air Reserve)	Maritime Patrol/Anti-Submarine Warfare	Broadarrows	Naval Air Station Jacksonville, Florida
US Naval Air Systems Command			
VX-20	Air Test & Evaluation	Force	Naval Air Station Patuxent River, Maryland

Since the days of the Orion, sensor, communications and weapon technology and performance had advanced dramatically. No longer would maritime patrol aircraft have to fly at low altitude - looking for submarine periscopes, controlling sonobuoy fields, and dropping depth charges.

So, the Poseidon was designed around sensors and weapons that could be used at medium altitude. This in turn meant that homing torpedoes were its main armament. The US Navy Mark 54 torpedo had to be modified so it could be employed at higher altitudes, to become the High-Altitude Anti-Submarine Warfare Weapon Capability »

LEFT: Sonobuoy dispensers underneath the P-8A's rear fuselage allow the acoustic devices to be sown to create fields to detect submarines over wider areas. (TIM RIPLEY)

BELOW: Up to 129 sonobuoys can be carried in built-in racks inside the P-8A's cabin. More can be carried in boxes in the cargo area of the aircraft, but this requires crew members to break them open before loading them. (US NAVY)

BAE Systems offered a version of its Nimrod MRA4 but soon dropped out. In 2004, Boeing won the competition for what was then called the Multi-Mission Maritime Aircraft, or MMA.

The Boeing aircraft became the P-8 Poseidon. Like the Orion before it, which was based on the Electra airliner, the Poseidon was derived from Boeing's best-selling 737 airliner. To make it suitable for maritime operations, the maker had to extensively modify the airliner's airframe and systems.

The P-8 is a militarised version of the 737-800ERX, a 737-800 with 737-900-based wings. The fuselage is similar to, but longer than, the 737-700-based C-40 Clipper transport aircraft in service with the US Navy. It has a strengthened fuselage for low-altitude operations and raked wingtips similar to those fitted to the Boeing 767-400ER, instead of the blended winglets available on 737NG variants.

At the heart of the Poseidon was a new concept of medium/high altitude anti-submarine operations.

RIGHT: Mission crews use common computer work stations to monitor the P-8A's acoustic, radar, electronic and optical sensors, as well as operating the aircraft's weapons. (US NAVY)

aircraft's tail, only work when an aircraft is flying directly over a submarine at low level. Without a MAD boom considerable weight and cost could be saved. A hydrocarbon sensor detects fuel vapours from diesel-powered submarines and ships.

Flight Crew

There is extensive automation throughout the P-8. The flight deck crew only required a pilot and co-pilot, with the flight engineer's position deleted. All the flight information is presented to the flight crew on large multi-function displays.

The main mission cabin has five work stations for sensor operators and mission specialists. These have a common computer architecture,

(HAAWC). A wing kit and a GPS guidance unit similar to those used by guided bombs was added to the torpedo so it could be precisely directed to a specific impact point. Without the wing kit to slow its decent, the torpedo would hit the water too fast and be damaged.

Getting the HAAWC to work was a major challenge and the development was plagued by technical problems, and it was only declared operational in November 2021, with production to start in 2024 out to 2030. The US Navy said it planned to buy 44 HAAWC systems.

The medium/high altitude operating profile meant that the traditional magnetic anomaly detector, or MAD boom, was not needed. MAD systems, which are usually installed underneath an

BELOW: The High Altitude Anti-Submarine Warfare Weapon Capability (HAAWC) allows torpedoes to be delivered from medium or high altitudes. It is essentially a glide bomb kit that is applied to a Mark 54 homing torpedo. (BOEING)

GLOBAL BOEING P-8A POSEIDON OPERATORS, JANUARY 2024	
Royal Australian Air Force	
11 Squadron	RAAF Base Edinburgh, South Australia
292 Squadron (Operational Conversion Unit)	RAAF Base Edinburgh, South Australia
12 × P-8A + 2 more on order	
Indian Navy	
Indian Naval Air Squadron 312	INS Rajali, Tamil Nadu
Indian Naval Air Squadron 316	INS Hansa, Goa
12 × P-8I	
Royal New Zealand Air Force	
No. 5 Squadron	RNZAF Base Ohakea
4 × P-8A	
Royal Norwegian Air Force	
333 Squadron	Evenes Air Station
5 × P-8A (incl 2 × aircraft based at NAS Jacksonville for training)	
Royal Air Force	
42 (Torpedo Bomber) Squadron	RAF Lossiemouth
120 Squadron	RAF Lossiemouth
201 Squadron	RAF Lossiemouth
9 × Poseidon MRA1	
Confirmed Future Operators	
German Naval Aviation	
Naval Air Wing 3 (MFG 3) "Graf Zeppelin"	Nordholz Naval Airbase
8 × P-8A	
Royal Canadian Air Force	
404 Long Range Patrol and Training Squadron	CFB Greenwood
405 Long Range Patrol Squadron	CFB Greenwood
415 Long Range Patrol Force Development Squadron	CFB Greenwood
407 Long Range Patrol Squadron	CFB Comox
16 × P-8A	
Republic of Korea Navy	
Patrol Squadron 61, 6th Air Wing	
6 × P-8A to be delivered by 2024	

BOEING P-8A POSEIDON

Crew: Nine

Capacity: 9,000kg (19,800lb)

Length: 39.47m (129ft 5in)

Wingspan: 37.64m (123ft 6in)

Height: 12.83m (42ft 1in)

Max take-off weight: 85,820kg (189,200lb)

Powerplant: Two × CFM56-7B27A turbofans

Cruise speed: 815kph (440kts)

Combat range: 2,225km (1,200nm)

Armament:

Internal bay with five hard-points and six external hardpoints for a variety of conventional weapons, AGM-84 Harpoon, AGM-84H/K SLAM-ER, AGM-88 AARGM-ER, AGM-158C LRASM, Mark 54 torpedo, naval mines, depth charges, and HAAWC

so each work station can view and access the same tactical information.

The aircraft has three rotary dispensers to sow sonobuoy fields in operation areas. Also, modern generations of sonobuoys can be re-programmed when they are in the sea to react to changing water conditions.

In addition to its Mk 54 homing torpedoes, the P-8 can carry Mk 82 depth charges in its bomb bay and up to six AGM-84 Harpoon anti-ship missiles can be carried on external hard points.

After receiving its development contract in 2004, the P-8 made its first flight in April 2009 and low-rate production was approved in August 2010. In March 2012, the first production aircraft was delivered to US Naval Air Station Jacksonville to allow the initial training and trials to take place. Full rate production was authorised in January 2014.

Production then started to ramp up and by July 2022 Boeing had delivered 119 aircraft to the US Navy. This was choreographed with the progressive retirement of the service's last P-3.

Boeing was also keen to promote the sale of P-8s to overseas customers. The main market was existing P-3 users, but Boeing made a major breakthrough in 2009 when India signed a contract for eight P-8I variants, which included many bespoke features including a MAD boom.

The same year, Australia selected the P-8 to replace its Orions and it signed a contract with the US Navy in 2012 and later expanded its order to 12 aircraft. Britain signed up to buy nine aircraft in 2016. Norway signed up later in 2017 to buy five aircraft and New Zealand ordered four in 2019. South Korea was the next customer in 2019 with an order for six aircraft. A further sale was signed in

2021 with Germany for five aircraft, which was expanded to eight in 2023. In November 2023 Canada announced it would buy up to 16 of the aircraft to replace its Lockheed CP-140 Auroras.

Sales campaigns are still underway, with Brazil, Denmark, Italy, Malaysia, Saudi Arabia, and Turkey all being linked as possible customers.

The US Navy has now re-equipped all its maritime patrol, or VP, squadrons with the P-8A. They are all home based at Jacksonville in Florida and Whidbey Island in Washington. For operations, P-8 detachments forward deploy to locations across the world to monitor potentially hostile submarine activity. These forward deployments are at Keflavik in Iceland, Lossiemouth in Scotland, Sigonella on Sicily, Bahrain in the Arabian Gulf, Kadena Air Base in Japan, Okinawa, and Kaneohe Bay Marine Corps Air Station on Hawaii.

ABOVE: After beginning its flight test programme in April 2009, the P-8A Poseidon finally replaced the P-3C in the US maritime patrol role in May 2020. The specialist P-3 variants are to be retired by 2025. (US NAVY)

BELOW: Naval Air Station Jacksonville is the home of the P-8A's that are dedicated to support US Navy and NATO operations in the North Atlantic, South America and Mediterranean theatres. It is also home to the Fleet Readiness Squadron or 'school house' for US Navy and allied P-8A crews. (US NAVY)

Magic Merlin

Britain's Anti-Submarine Helicopter

ABOVE: Royal Navy Merlin HM2 maritime helicopters provide anti-submarine protection for Britain's two Queen Elizabeth-class aircraft carriers. (MOD/CROWN COPYRIGHT)

In the 1970s, the Royal Navy began looking to replace its veteran Sea King anti-submarine helicopter. The Yeovil-based helicopter company, Westland, had begun building the iconic Sea King for the British armed forces in 1969 and it then started to modify the helicopter for the unique requirements of the Royal Navy.

British Sea Kings started to feature home grown radars, sonobuoy dispensers, dipping sonar, communications, and a central computer system to control all this technology. This meant the final anti-submarine versions of the Sea King were highly capable, but the air frame was being pushed to the limit, reducing the performance and endurance of the helicopter.

The answer was the Merlin. Britain's Westland joined forces with Italy's Agusta to build a new helicopter to replace both country's maritime Sea Kings. It was slightly bigger than a Sea King so could carry more fuel and could spend more time on station. The new helicopter also had three engines so it could fly faster but, more importantly, it could carry more weapons, sensors, and anti-submarine equipment.

Making all the systems on the helicopter work together was a crucial to the project and the Royal Navy wanted to incorporate a high degree of computerised automation so the crew size could be reduced. The ambition was to have one observer working the anti-submarine systems, as well as two flight crew. During intensive sub-hunting operations, the co-pilot could move to the rear cabin to help the observer monitor the sensors or re-load the sonobuoy dispenser.

To ensure effective system integration the American company IBM-Aerospace Systems Integration, which subsequently became Loral and is now Lockheed Martin, was designated the prime contractor to run the project to deliver 44 Merlin HM1s helicopter for the Royal Navy.

The Merlin HM1 main sensors were a Thomson-Marconi active 'dipping' sonar to give enhanced submarine detection ranges and a Marconi Blue Kestrel radar which provided full 360° coverage of surface targets, such as ships or submarine periscopes. It could also pass tactical information via an automated datalink to other helicopters, aircraft, or ships.

The Merlin can be armed with four Stingray homing anti-submarine torpedoes and Mk 11 depth charges.

Upgrades to the Merlin have been underway since 2000. In 2007 an urgent operational requirement project fitted an MX-15 electro-optical

RIGHT: From 2010 to 2020 the Royal Navy's Merlin HM2s were Britain's sole anti-submarine aircraft after the scrapping of the RAF's Nimrod MRA4 project. (MOD/CROWN COPYRIGHT)

video camera turret and defensive aid suite to Merlins operating in the Arabian Gulf region.

The Royal Navy launched a major upgrade to modernise the helicopter, dubbed the Merlin Capability Sustainment Plus (MCSP). Lockheed Martin UK was selected to be the lead integrator for the £750m MSCP, which incorporated open architecture computer systems into the helicopters with improved processing power, added new capabilities for the Blue Kestrel radar and sonar system, better datalinks, and upgraded the aircrew consoles and avionics, including large flat panel touch screens. On a tactical level, these improvements enabled 40 times the number of targets to be tracked compared to the Merlin HM1's systems, improved submarine detection in shallow water, and enhanced night operations. While improved capabilities flowed from these upgrades, the primary goal was to resolve electronics obsolescence issues and keep the helicopter flying out to 2040, as well as reducing the through life support and operating costs. The MCSP helicopters were designated the HM2, and the first ones were ready for frontline service from 2014. Only 30 Merlins were upgraded to the new standard.

The Italian Navy also ordered a maritime variant of the Merlin, but it featured many different systems, including T-700-GE-T6A1 engines, Eliradar APS-784 radar and Honeywell HELRAS dipping sonar. They are armed with torpedoes or Marte anti-ship missiles.

The home of the Fleet Air Arm's three operational Naval Air Squadrons (NAS) equipped with the Merlin HM2 is RNAS Culdrose, which is officially titled HMS *Sea Hawk*.

Training and Overhaul

As well as the Merlin squadrons, Culdrose is also home to a simulator centre to train Merlin air crew and a maintenance facility where contractors from Leonardo (formerly Westland) overhaul the helicopters. The two core Merlin HM2 units, 814 and 820 NAS, spend their time detached to Royal Navy warships providing anti-submarine protection and surface surveillance.

The 2010 defence review scrapped the RAF's BAE Systems Nimrod MRA4 maritime patrol aircraft project, leaving the Fleet Air Arm Merlin HM2s as Britain's only airborne anti-submarine platform. They were routinely deployed to Prestwick International Airport in Ayrshire to fly security patrols to protect the arrival and departure of Britain's Vanguard-class nuclear deterrent submarines from their base at Faslane on the Clyde. During this period, many ex-Nimrod RAF personnel re-mustered to the Royal Navy to bolster the Merlin squadrons.

After the Royal Navy's two new Queen Elizabeth-class aircraft carriers joined the fleet from 2017, the Merlin HMS2 squadrons returned to their traditional role operating from carriers as the anti-submarine screen around naval task groups.

In 2021, HMS *Queen Elizabeth* sailed to the Far East for a major deployment and her embarked Merlin HM2s duelled with Chinese submarines operating around the Royal Navy task group. During 2024, HMS *Queen Elizabeth* will begin a period of extended maintenance and sister ship, HMS *Prince of Wales* will take over as the high readiness carrier. She is to sail back to the Far East and will have Merlin HM2s embarked. »

ABOVE: The Merlin HM2 has a Thales FLASH dipping sonar to complement its sonobuoys for underwater surveillance. (MOD/CROWN COPYRIGHT, VIA LEONARDO)

BELOW: The BAE Systems Stingray homing torpedo is the Merlin HM2's main submarine killing weapon. (MOD/CROWN COPYRIGHT)

The Merlin Force 2024

RIGHT: The Leonardo Blue Kestrel 5000 maritime surveillance radar allows Royal Navy Merlin HM2 crews to monitor wide areas of sea, including picking up submarine periscopes or snorkels. (MOD/CROWN COPYRIGHT)

814 Naval Air Squadron

The arrival of the Westland Merlin HM1 saw the squadron reformed in 2001 to operate the advanced ASW helicopter. It subsequently re-equipped with the upgraded AgustaWestland Merlin HM2 in 2014. Personnel from the disbanded 829 Naval Air Squadron were incorporated into the unit in 2018, and 814 Squadron took over its role to supply independent flights on frigates and destroyers. It also regularly deploys to Faslane in Scotland.

814 NAVAL AIR SQUADRON
Home Station: RNAS Culdrose
Current Aircraft: AgustaWestland Merlin HM2
First formed: 1938
Nickname: The Flying Tigers

BELOW: Merlin HM2s of 814 Naval Air Squadron have the role of supplying independent flights on Royal Navy frigates and destroyers. (MOD/CROWN COPYRIGHT)

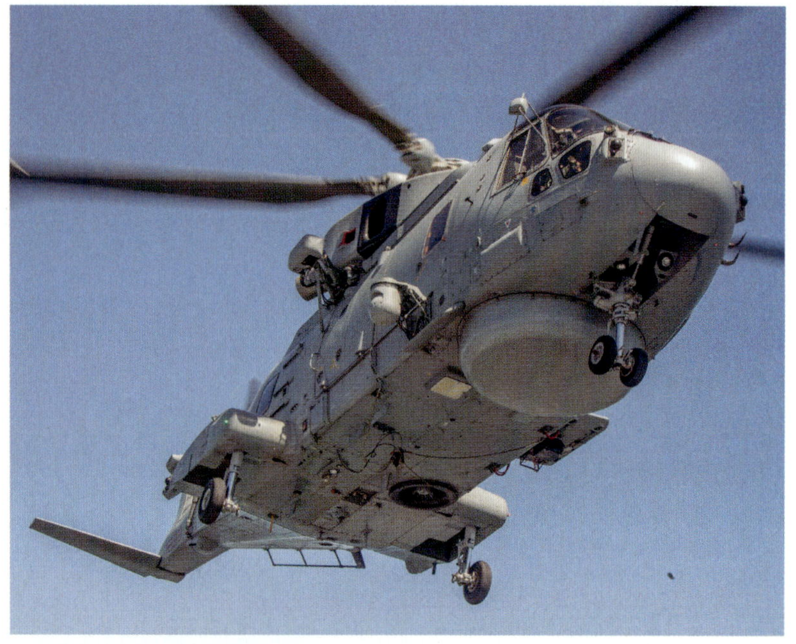

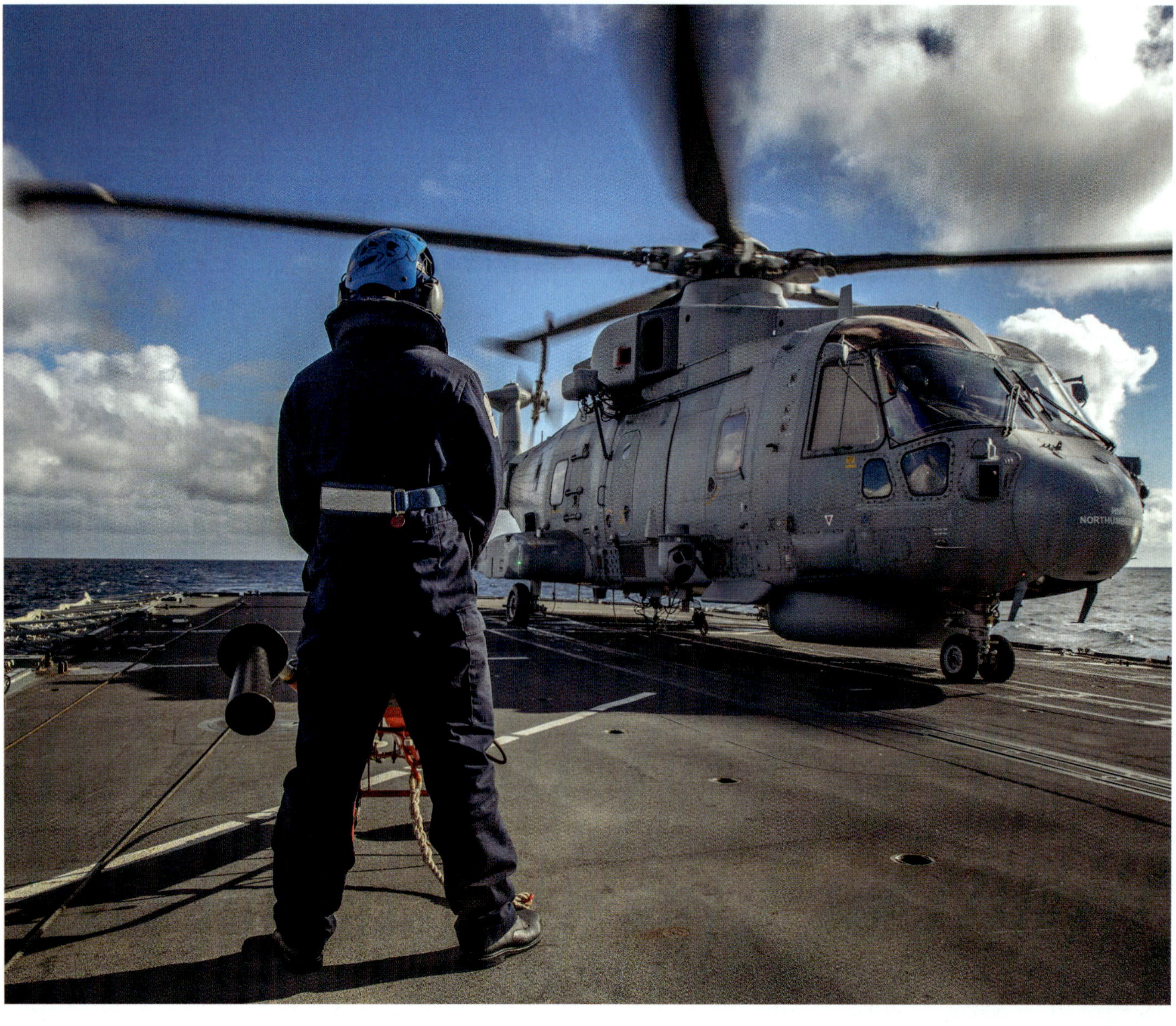

MERLIN HM2		
Crew: Three		
Powerplant: Three × Rolls-Royce Turbomeca RTM322-01 turboshaft engines		
Max take-off weight: 14,600kg (32,187lb)		
Cruise speed: 278kph (173mph, 150kts)		
Range: 833km (518 miles, 450nm)		
Endurance: Five hours		
Avionics:		
Selex Galileo Blue Kestrel 5000 maritime surveillance radar		
Active/passive sonobuoys		
Thales 2189 dipping sonar array		
Armament:		
Bombs: Four × Stingray homing torpedoes or Mk 11 depth charges		
Door guns: One x .50cal machine gun		

LEFT: Small ship detachments of Merlin HM2s have to be prepared to carry out many secondary roles, in addition to their primary anti-submarine mission. (MOD/CROWN COPYRIGHT)

820 Naval Air Squadron

From 2001 onwards it has operated both versions of the anti-submarine Merlin helicopter and it is now the core helicopter squadron for HMS *Queen Elizabeth*'s air group, hence her nickname, The Queen's Squadron. The squadron embarked on the carrier for her maiden operational Carrier Strike Group deployment to the Far East in 2021.

820 NAVAL AIR SQUADRON	
Home Station: RNAS Culdrose	
Current Aircraft: AgustaWestland Merlin HM2	
First formed: 1933	
Nickname: The Queen's Squadron	

824 Naval Air Squadron

824 was an old sea squadron and disbanded in 1989, it reformed in 2000 with the Westland Merlin HM1. It initially provided helicopters to operate as independent flights on frigates and destroyers. The unit's Merlins were named after knights of King Arthur's famous round table.

It is now the main Merlin training unit, preparing pilots, observers, aircrew, and ground crew to operate the helicopter in a dedicated training facility at RNAS Culdrose that is equipped with purpose-built simulators.

824 NAVAL AIR SQUADRON	
Home Station: RNAS Culdrose	
Current Aircraft: AgustaWestland Merlin HM2	
First formed: 1933	

LEFT: 814 Naval Air Squadron is nicknamed the 'Flying Tigers'. (TIM RIPLEY)

Astute

The Royal Navy's Hunter Killers

Britain was the third nation to commission a nuclear-powered attack submarine, HMS *Dreadnought* was laid down in 1959 and commissioned in 1963. Since then, the Royal Navy has placed nuclear attack boats at the heart of its operations and during the Cold War they were used aggressively to locate and track Soviet submarines in the North Atlantic.

In 1992, the Royal Navy decided to phase out its conventionally powered submarines and move to an all nuclear-powered fleet. It proposed building a new class of attack boats that would incorporate new digital technology and significantly enhanced underwater sensors. The new Astute-class would be optimised to hunt and kill enemy submarines.

Today, it boasts a fleet of six attack boats – five Astute-class and one remaining Trafalgar-class – and has two more Astute-class on order, for delivery by 2026.

The modern Astute-class are very different from the Churchill-class boats of the 1980s. HMS *Conqueror* weighed 4,900 tons when submerged and its modern counterpart comes in at 7,800 tons. The Astute class have far more capable weapons, including US-made Tomahawk Land Attack Missiles (TLAMs) that can hit targets thousands of kilometres inland and Spearfish homing torpedoes. Her acoustic sensors can detect targets at thousands of kilometres range thanks to dramatic improvements in computing power since the 1980s. The most obvious difference is that the modern submarine does not have a traditional periscope. During the

1981 Falklands war, Commander Chris Wreford-Brown, of HMS *Conqueror*, personally had to detect and identify the ARA *General Belgrano*, using a periscope that was little different to those used in World War Two. His modern successors benefit from periscopes that are essentially digital television cameras that can stream video images they collect to multiple workstations in the submarine's command centre.

The Astute-class boasts far more capable sonar than its Cold War-era predecessors to enable it to detect submarines and ships at very long distances. One senior Royal Navy

officer boasted that an Astute submarine in UK waters would be able to 'hear' a merchant vessel leaving New York harbour. He added that submarines were more challenging but claimed that Russian boats could be picked up at 50 to 60 nautical miles range.

Each Astute-class boat has a Sonar 2076 system, which comprises an integrated suite of active and passive sonar systems including bow, fin, flank, and towed arrays.

BAE Systems, which is responsible for building the Astute-class submarines and integrating the Type 2076 Sonar, claims that it represents a 'step change' over previous sonars and is the world's most advanced and effective sonar system. It reportedly comprises 13,000 individual hydrophones, many times the number fitted in previous Royal Navy systems and more than any other submarine sonar in service. When it was designed in the mid-1990s its processing power was said to be equivalent to 60,000 home PCs. Upgrades since then have made it even more capable.

The crews of Astute-class submarines also live in significantly

ASTUTE CLASS SUBMARINE FLEET - SEPTEMBER 2023					
Name	Pennant	Laid down	Launched	Commissioned	Status
HMS Astute	S119	31-Jan-01	08-Jun-07	27-Aug-10	Active service
HMS Ambush	S120	22-Oct-03	06-Jan-11	01-Mar-13	Active service
HMS Artful	S121	11-Mar-05	17-May-14	18-Mar-16	Active service
HMS Audacious	S122	24-Mar-09	28-Apr-17	03-Apr-20	Under repair at Devonport
HMS Anson	S123	13-Oct-11	20-Apr-21	31-Aug-22	Sea trials
HMS Agamemnon	S124	18-Jul-13			Under construction
HMS Agincourt	S125	14-May-18			Under construction

improved conditions. Unlike on HMS *Conqueror*, every member of their crews has their own bunk to sleep in. On the older boats so-called 'hot bunking' was the norm, even on cruises that lasted several months.

Nuclear Progression

Back in 1963 Britain's first nuclear boat, HMS *Dreadnought* boasted a US-supplied nuclear reactor, and it was three years before a submarine, HMS *Valiant*, with a British built reactor was commissioned.

In the 1990s the Royal Navy began ordering the current generation of Astute-class submarines and they incorporated many improvements over the Trafalgar-class and Swiftsure-class they were to replace. The Astute-class were the first British submarines of the modern computer era and featured communication systems that allowed them to operate in close co-ordination with surface ships, strike aircraft, and special forces.

In 1999, the Royal Navy entered a new era when the Swiftsure-class submarine, HMS *Splendid*, fired Tomahawk cruise missiles at Serbian targets during the Kosovo conflict. More cruise missiles were fired during the 2001 Afghan, 2003 Iraq and 2011 Libyan conflicts. British submarines were now strategic »

BELOW: HMS *Audacious* alongside at the US Naval Base at Souda Bay in Crete during her extended deployment in the Mediterranean in 2022. (MOD/CROWNCOPYRIGHT)

RIGHT: HMS *Ambush* is the second submarine of the Astute-class, and she entered service in 2013. (MOD/CROWN COPYRIGHT)

strike assets that could contribute to air and land operations.

The Astute-class may have represented a quantum advance in capability over previous attack submarines but bringing them into service severely stretched its builders, BAE Systems. HMS *Astute* was ordered in 1997 and was not launched until 2007. It took a further three years for her to be commissioned in 2010 but not formally declared fully ready for operations until 2014. The cost of the first three Astute-class boats escalated by 58% to over £3.5bn. As result of the lessons learned with the first three boats of this class, the last four submarines are

incorporating many improvements to make them easier to build and enhance their operational capabilities. This has meant these four submarines are expected to cost more than £5bn to build, making them the most expensive submarines ever built for the Royal Navy.

The first of class, HMS *Astute*, seemed to be jinxed. She ran aground, resulting in her captain being relieved of duty and then in 2011 a drunken sailor ran amok with a rifle, killing an officer and wounding two other sailors. More problems hit the fourth boat, HMS *Audacious,* during her construction. It took more than 12 years from being laid down in 2009 to her entering service. This was attributed to her containing so many new systems and equipment, that she was essentially a first of class. The COVID-19 pandemic also hit the Barrow-in-Furness shipyard hard just as she was near completion.

The Submarine Service turned a major corner in 2022 with HMS *Audacious* finally coming online and HMS *Anson* arriving at Faslane to

begin her acceptance and work up trials. This allowed the retirement in May 2022 of HMS *Trenchant* and HMS *Talent*, which left only HMS *Triumph* in service as the final Trafalgar-class boat. Once HMS *Anson* is fully

ASTUTE-CLASS NUCLEAR-POWERED ATTACK SUBMARINE

Complement: 98 (capacity for 109)

Displacement submerged: 7,800 tons

Length: 97m (318ft 3in)

Beam: 11.3m (37ft 1in)

Draught: 10m (32ft 10in)

Propulsion: One × Rolls-Royce PWR 2 nuclear reactor

Speed: 56kph (30kts), submerged

Armament:

Six × 21in (533mm) torpedo tubes with stowage for up to 38 weapons, including combination of Tomahawk Block IV cruise missiles and Spearfish heavyweight torpedoes

BELOW: Royal Navy Astute-class submarines regularly practice deploying contingents of UK and allied special forces troops covertly on enemy coast lines. (MOD/CROWN COPYRIGHT)

operational and HMS *Agamemnon* is in the water in 2025, it is expected that HMS *Triumph* will finally be retired after nearly 35 years of service.

HMS *Astute* played a prominent part in the Carrier Strike Group 2021 deployment to the Far East and during her six-month deployment made port calls in South Korea and Australia, both firsts for Royal Navy nuclear attack submarines.

The links established during HMS *Astute*'s visits to the Far East played an important part in the first phases of the Australia-US-UK submarine deal and further visits to Australia by Royal Navy submarines are expected to become more frequent over the coming decade as the country starts to build its own attack boats, using technology from the Astute-class.

The Astute-class boats are now earning their keep as the core of the Submarine Service, carrying out routine patrols in the North Atlantic and further afield. In early 2022, one unidentified boat operated in Norwegian coastal waters, covertly delivering Royal Marine reconnaissance teams close to shore targets during NATO exercises.

HMS *Audacious* was forward deployed to the Mediterranean for 353 days up to April 2023 to take part in exercises with NATO allies and other partner navies. She operated temporarily from ports on Cyprus and Crete during this deployment. In a first, the submarine was docked in Cyprus over the Christmas period and her crew's families joined them on the island for the festivities.

A major challenge for the Ministry of Defence is the safe storage and disposal of the 22 nuclear-power submarines that have been retired from Royal Navy service. They are currently stored at Rosyth and Devonport dockyards, awaiting disposal. Work is underway to plan how to compete the de-fuelling of the submarine's reactors and then to finally take the redundant boats out of the water and break them up. Progress has been slow because of wider national issues over the disposal of nuclear waste.

ABOVE: HMS *Audacious* under construction in the Devonshire Hall Dock in Barrow-in-Furness. (BAE SYSTEMS)

BELOW: HMS *Audacious* operated under NATO command during her extended deployment in the Mediterranean in **2022.** (MOD/CROWNCOPYRIGHT)

SH-60 Seahawk

America's Sub Hunting Helicopter

RIGHT: An MH-60R Sea Hawk of Helicopter Maritime Strike Squadron (HSM) 71 prepares to land aboard the aircraft carrier USS *John C. Stennis*, as the guided-missile destroyer USS *Chung* follows behind during a 'show of force' transit close to Taiwan. (US NAVY)

America's primary anti-submarine helicopter is the Sikorsky SH-60R Seahawk, which operates from US Navy warships to protect naval task forces.

The Seahawk shares a common heritage with the US Army's famous UH-60 Blackhawk, but it has been extensively modified to operate in the maritime environment.

Development of the SH-60 began in the 1970s as a replacement for the Kaman SH-2 Seasprite, which was the main maritime helicopter operated from US Navy frigates and warships to fill the Light Airborne Multi-Purpose System (LAMPS) requirement. The helicopter incorporated unique features to allow it to operate on ships, including folding main rotor blades and a folding tail.

The first Seahawk variant, the SH-60B, entered service with the US Navy in 1984 and it featured specialist anti-submarine equipment, including a magnetic anomaly detector (MAD) and sonobuoy dispensers. A variant was licence produced in Japan.

During the late 1980s, the US Navy turned to the SH-60 to replace its veteran Sikorsky SH-3 Sea King as the main anti-submarine helicopter embarked on US aircraft carriers. The SH-60F first flew in 1987 and

BELOW: Helicopter Anti-Submarine Squadron (HS) 11 operated the SH-60F Seahawk anti-submarine variant up to 2016. (US NAVY)

SIKORSKY SH-60 SEAHAWK	
Crew: Three to four	
Capacity: Five passengers in cabin	
Length: 64ft 8in (19.71m)	
Height: 17ft 2in (5.23m)	
Gross weight: 17,758lb (8,055kg) for ASW mission	
Powerplant: Two × General Electric T700-GE-401C turboshaft engines	
Maximum speed: 146kts (168mph, 270 kph)	
Range: 450nm (520 miles, 830km)	
Armament:	
Two Mk 46, Mk 50, or Mk 54 torpedoes	

SH-60/S-70B FOREIGN OPERATORS

Australia
• 23 MH-60R Seahawks, with 12 on order

Brazil
• 8 S-70B Seahawks

Denmark
• 9 MH-60R Seahawks

Greece
• 12 S-70B6 Aegean Hawks

India
• 5 MH-60R Seahawks and 19 more on order

Israel
• 8 on order

Japan
• 80+ SH-60J/K remain in service

South Korea
• 8 S-70/UH-60P and 12 MH-60R on order

Saudi Arabia
• 10 MH-60R

Singapore
• 8 S-70 Seahawks

Spain
• 22 SH-60B/Fs

Taiwan (Republic of China)
• 9 S-70C(M)-1 and 10 S-70C(M)-2

Thailand
• 6 S-70B and 2 MH-60S Seahawks

Turkey
• 24 S-70 Seahawks

LEFT: The SH-60F Seahawk anti-submarine variant was equipped with the Bendix AN/AQS-13Fdipping sonar. (US NAVY)

LEFT: The original Seahawk variant the SH-60B, served with US Navy Helicopter Anti-Submarine Light (HSL) unit up to 2015. (US NAVY)

its additional systems included an AQS-13F dipping sonar and it carried a six-tube sonobuoy launcher.

More recently, the US Navy has sought to rationalise its SH-60 variants and developed the SH-60R, or Romeo. This combined the features of the SH-60B and SH-60F in a single airframe. These included AN/APS-153 multi-mode surface surveillance radar with Automatic Radar Periscope Detection and Discrimination (ARPDD) features, AN/AQS-22 low-frequency dipping sonar, magnetic anomaly detector, sonobuoy dispenser, as well as integrating Mk-54 homing torpedoes and Hellfire anti-ship missiles into its arsenal.

The SH-60R first entered service in 2006 and by 2015 had fully replaced B and F variants in US Navy Helicopter Anti-Submarine Light (HSL) and Helicopter Antisubmarine Squadrons (HS). The Romeo variants are now operated by Helicopter, Strike Maritime (HSM) squadrons. Each US aircraft carrier now embarks an HSM squadron and smaller warships embark expeditionary detachments. In total, 166 SH-60Rs are now operated by the US Navy.

The SH-60 has been widely exported and some 14 air arms around the world operate the helicopter, often using the designation S-70B Seahawk. The helicopter is still in production for export customers, with a configuration similar to the SH-60R.

Despite being in service for almost 40 years, SH-60 variants have never seen combat against hostile submarines or claimed any kills. However, it has proved a robust and reliable aircraft that is popular with its crews. US SH-60Rs are the most capable anti-submarine variant yet but this results in the rear cabin being very full of mission equipment, which limits its ability to carry cargo and passengers in the utility role.

Poseidon MRA1

The RAF's Kipper Fleet Reborn

A s first missions go it was a gentle baptism of fire. The Russian corvette, the RFS *Vasily Bykov,* had entered the North Sea and 120, or CXX, Squadron was tasked with finding the ship. A Boeing Poseidon MRA1 was launched from the squadron's temporary base at Kinloss Barracks in Moray on August 7, 2020, and in less than an hour the Russian ship was in view. For several hours, the RAF jet shadowed the *Vasily Bykov* before the aircraft returned to its Scottish base.

A week later, CXX Squadron found itself called in to action again in very different circumstances. Migrants were attempting to cross the English Channel in inflatable boats in ever increasing numbers. By early August 2020, the UK Border Force asked for military help to monitor the waterway. The first aircraft on patrol on August 10 was an Airbus A400M transport, which was on alert as the national standby aircraft at RAF Brize Norton, but its crew had little in the way of surveillance equipment except for binoculars. A more capable aircraft was needed so on August 12, a Poseidon was launched from Kinloss to fly up and down the Channel.

The RAF was now back in the maritime patrol game after a 10-year capability gap. It was fitting that CXX Squadron flew its first missions from the former RAF Kinloss, which is now a British Army base, where the last Hawker Siddeley Nimrod MR2 served until their premature retirement in March 2010. The runway and other airport facilities were retained at Kinloss Barracks to allow it to act as

a temporary operating site for nearby RAF Lossiemouth in emergencies.

The renaissance of the Kipper Fleet, as the Nimrod Force and before them RAF Coastal Command had been nicknamed, had its origins in the November 2015 Strategic Defence and Security Review, which recognised that the lack of maritime patrol aircraft was a key capability gap that needed to be addressed. Plans to buy

LEFT: The first RAF Poseidon relocated to their permanent home at RAF Lossiemouth in October 2020, after temporarily operating from nearby Kinloss Barracks. The first Poseidon arrived at the former RAF Kinloss on February 4, 2020, to begin the rebuilding of the RAF's maritime patrol capability after the retirement of the Nimrod MR2 a decade earlier. (MOD/CROWN COPYRIGHT)

nine Poseidon aircraft for the RAF were approved by Prime Minister David Cameron.

The formal title of the project is officially the UK Persistent Wide Area Surveillance – Maritime (PWAS-M), and it was needed to meet an 'urgent anti-submarine-warfare-driven requirement'. The target for an initial operational capability (IOC) of two aircraft was set for April 2020 to deliver aircraft with both anti-submarine warfare (ASW) and anti-surface warfare capabilities.

Procurement activity accelerated in March 2017 when the first contracts for production of aircraft for the United Kingdom were placed as part of a batch of 17 aircraft for the US Navy. The delivery schedule envisaged all nine aircraft being handed over between the spring of 2020 and early 2022.

The RAF has a long history of maritime patrol operations stretching back to the Second World War when Coastal Command played a key role in defeating Nazi U-Boats during the Battle of the Atlantic. During the Cold War, RAF Nimrod crews regularly won plaudits for their anti-submarine warfare skills. RAF crews won the UK–Canada–New Zealand–Australia Fincastle Trophy ASW skills competition 18 times out of the 43 occasions it was held up to 2008. Bringing the Poseidon into service requires different skills to those perfected by the old Nimrod community, with RAF officers involved in the Poseidon programme repeatedly telling audiences, "This is not a new Nimrod."

The P-8A boasts many of the traditional features of a maritime patrol aircraft, including the ability to launch and control sonobuoys to find and monitor submarines and other underwater threats. It features an AN/APY-10 surface surveillance radar and forward-looking infrared sensor turret and can be armed with Mk 54 Lightweight Hybrid Torpedoes (LHTs) and AGM-84 Harpoon II anti-ship missiles. The aircraft's mission systems are fully digital, allowing wide area surveillance and enhanced network connectivity with other air, land, and marine assets.

New RAF squadrons have been formed to operate the United Kingdom's Poseidon, the first stood up in April 2018. Wing Commander James Hanson oversaw the formation of CXX Squadron, while the second unit, 201 Squadron, was stood up in August 2021. Both of these units operated the Nimrod MR2 before the aircraft was retired and have »

BELOW: All nine Poseidon aircraft were handed over to the RAF by early 2022. (MOD/CROWN COPYRIGHT)

ABOVE: The RAF Poseidon squadrons share RAF Lossiemouth with four RAF Typhoon fighter squadrons. (MOD/CROWN COPYRIGHT)

BELOW: Ready to go. The first RAF Poseidon touched down at Kinloss Barracks on February 4, 2020. (MOD/CROWN COPYRIGHT)

base at RAF Lossiemouth. Eventually the aim is to have 18 Poseidon crews to operate its nine aircraft when full operation capability is declared in 2024. Five crews had been trained by early 2022.

The start of UK Poseidon operational conversion training was a major milestone in the RAF programme to regenerate a maritime patrol aircraft capability, running in parallel with assembly work starting on the first UK aircraft. The first two UK Poseidons operated from Kinloss Barracks until runway repairs at RAF Lossiemouth were completed in October 2020 to allow them to move to their permanent home.

The first UK Poseidon, ZP801, now named *Pride of Moray*, was handed over to the RAF in October 2019 and it flew to Kinloss on February 4, 2020.

The RAF Poseidon programme included not just the procurement of the aircraft but also encompasses the training for aircrew and maintenance personnel, as well as support infrastructure at RAF Lossiemouth.

This project is part of the wider Lossiemouth Development Plan

a strong tradition of maritime patrol stretching back to the Coastal Command days.

US Training

The first RAF frontline crews and maintenance personnel entered training at the US Navy Poseidon school house at Naval Air Station (NAS) Jacksonville in Florida in January 2019. Thirty-eight RAF personnel of CXX Squadron arrived in the US to begin operational conversion training. This involved the first fully formed UK crew to undergo training in the US, with previous RAF personnel being trained at NAS Jacksonville to gain experience of

the Poseidon as individuals seconded to US Navy units under Project Seedcorn. This was initiated after the scrapping of the Nimrod MR2 and its successor, the Nimrod MRA4, in a bid to retain vital maritime patrol skills and expertise in the RAF by posting personnel to the US Navy, Royal Australian Air Force, Royal New Zealand Air Force, and Royal Canadian Air Force.

The ramp-up of the UK Poseidon training effort initially took place at NAS Jacksonville before the Poseidon training organisation moved to the UK in late 2021 following the installation of a set of simulators at the future Poseidon main operating

POSEIDON NAMES

All the RAF Poseidon aircraft will bear names linking them to the Moray area, RAF Lossiemouth, or have historic significance to the RAF maritime patrol community.

ZP801 *Pride of Moray*
ZP802 *City of Elgin*
ZP803 *Terence Bulloch DSO* DFC**
ZP804 *Spirit of Reykjavik*
ZP805 *Fulmar*
ZP806 *Guernsey's Reply*
ZP807 *William Barker VC*
ZP808 not yet named
ZP809 not yet named

POSEIDON MRA1

In service: 2020 to date

Used by: Royal Air Force

Manufacturer: Boeing

Produced: 2009 onwards

Number built: Nine

Specifications

Powerplant: Two × CFM56-7B27A turbofans

Length: 39.47m (129ft 5in)

Wingspan: 37.64m (123ft 6in)

Height: 12.83m (42ft 1in)

Max take-off weight: 85,820kg (189,200lb)

Maximum speed: 907kph (490kts)

Combat range: 2,222km (1,200nm)

Crew: Nine

Avionics:

Raytheon APY-10 multi-mission surface search radar

AN/APS-154 Advanced Airborne Sensor

Armament:

AGM-84 Harpoon, Mark 54 torpedo, mines, depth charges, and possibly the High-Altitude Anti-Submarine Warfare Weapon Capability (HAAWC) system

which is being managed by the UK Defence Infrastructure Organisation (DIO). The new Poseidon Strategic Facility, now formally known as the Atlantic Building, includes a tactical operations centre, facilities for an operational conversion unit, squadron accommodation, training and simulation facilities, and a three-bay aircraft hangar.

The dedicated P-8A simulation centre houses simulators including two flight deck crew operational flight trainers (OFTs) and weapons tactics trainers (WTTs) to train rear-cabin mission crew.

The RAF's Kipper Fleet is now firmly back in business and the UK's maritime patrol capability gap that opened with the retirement of the Nimrod MR2 in 2010, is now being closed. For the foreseeable future, the RAF's new King of the Sea will be patrolling around Britain's coasts.

ABOVE: The purpose-built Atlantic Building at RAF Lossiemouth is the home of all UK Poseidon operations, training, and maintenance. (MOD/CROWN COPYRIGHT)

BELOW: RAF Lossiemouth's runways and taxiways have been substantially upgraded to accommodate the RAF Poseidon fleet. (MOD/CROWN COPYRIGHT)

Type 23
Britain's Sub Hunting Frigates

ABOVE: HMS *Somerset* on an anti-submarine patrol in the North Atlantic, showing off the classic lines of the Type 23 class. (MOD/CROWNCOPYRIGHT)

Britain's Royal Navy has more than 80 years' experience of operating submarine hunting vessels and its current Type 23, Duke-class, frigates incorporate many specialist features to reduce their sound signature and enhance their ability to find and kill their underwater adversary.

The Type 23 general purpose frigates are often described as the 'workhorse of the Royal Navy'. The II surviving Royal Navy Type 23s are the service's most reliable and effective surface vessels.

The Type 23 originated at the height of the Cold War in the early 1980s and were designed by the Royal Corps of Naval Constructors (RCNC). From the start the Royal Navy wanted the future Type 23 to lead its anti-submarine warfare operations in the North Atlantic to counter the growing Soviet submarine threat. Every piece of machinery, as well as doors and mechanical devices on the ship is fitted with devices to reduce their vibration or other noises.

It would be the first Royal Navy warship to be designed from the start to be equipped with towed sonar arrays, which in the early 1980s were seen as the key to outsmarting the latest generation of ultra-quiet Soviet submarines. By trailing the sonar array thousands of metres behind the frigate, it is moved away from

the noise generated by the ship's engines and machinery. This allows sonar operators to pick up the sound of enemy submarines at very long distances, giving them a crucial tactical advantage.

Sonar 2087 is described by its manufacturer as "a towed-array system that enables Type 23 frigates to hunt the latest submarines at considerable distances and locate them beyond the range at which they [submarines] can launch an attack."

It is a Low Frequency Active Sonar and consists of both active and passive sonar arrays. Sonar 2087 was fitted to eight Type 23 frigates in mid-life refits between 2004 and 2012; the five oldest Type 23 frigates, HMS *Montrose*, *Monmouth*, *Iron Duke*, *Lancaster*, and *Argyll* have not received Sonar 2087.

Sonar 2087 (sometimes shortened to S2087) is designed and manufactured by Thales Underwater Systems. It replaces the older Sonar 2031 in the Royal Navy, and the system is also to

RIGHT: The Type 2087 towed sonar array is stowed in bays at the rear of Type 23 frigates when not in use. (MOD/CROWNCOPYRIGHT)

equip the Royal Navy's future Type 26 frigates.

The Type 23s with the Type 2087 sonar are generally kept in European waters to counter Russian submarines and ships without the new sonar were deployed on more far-ranging missions to operational theatres with a less intense submarine threat.

The Type 23's own noise signature in turn is reduced by its combined diesel-electric and gas (CODLAG) propulsion system, which provides incredibly quiet running for anti-submarine operations. This allows the electric motors to take over the mechanical propulsion to reduce vibration. The electric propulsion is powered by diesel generators that are positioned above the waterline and acoustically shielded. Its propellers are also designed to suppress cavitation, again to reduce the ship's acoustic signature.

Prior to operational cruises, the Type 23 frigates are sent to the Loch Goil and Lock Fyne sound ranges to test their acoustic signatures and identify sources of noise within the ships. The ship's crews can then take action to reduce their sound signature.

Operational Options

After a submarine is detected and its location pinpointed by a Type 23, the frigate has a number of weapon options to kill them. The

BAE Systems Stingray homing torpedo can be fired from the ship's twin launchers or dropped from its AgustaWestland Wildcat HMA2 or Merlin HM2 helicopters. It can also drop Mk 11 depth charges. The Royal Navy's Wildcats have a surface surveillance capability from their Leonardo Sea Spray radar and L-3 Wescam MX-15HDi electro-

optical/infrared nose turret but no underwater detection capability. So, the helicopter's crew can only launch their anti-submarine weapons on the directions of their parent ship.

The Type 23s replaced three existing classes of frigates – the Leanders, Type 21 and Type 22s – in a bid to dramatically reduce training, logistic and support costs. The 1970s era »

ABOVE: HMS *Argyll* in the Devonport Frigate Refit facility for a maintenance period in 2022, as part of an ongoing effort to keep the anti-submarine systems on the Type 23s up to date with current threats. (BABCOCK)

BELOW: Although Royal Navy Type 23 frigates have a primary anti-submarine role, they are also armed with weapons, such as anti-ship missiles, to take on surface targets. (MOD/CROWNCOPYRIGHT)

Frigate Refit Complex in Devonport dockyard has since modernised and been transformed into the centre of excellence for the overhaul and upgrade of Type 23 frigates.

During their life, the Type 23s have been progressively upgraded, with new weapons, sensors and other equipment being installed at regular intervals. The early ships of the class, which were laid down in the late 1980s, are starting to show their age and are now in urgent need of being replaced when the new Type 26 frigates come on line later this decade. Under current plans the last Type 23, HMS *St Albans*, will not retire before 2035.

The Type 23 upgrade programme is dubbed the Life Extension, or LIFEX, and it involves the installation of the Sea Ceptor air defence missile to replace the old Sea Wolf weapons as well as a power generation machinery upgrade. This latter upgrade involves the replacement of four generators with more modern equipment that makes the ships more efficient.

In 2019 the first Type 23s started to receive the new Martlet close-in anti-ship missiles which are designed to counter swarms of fast patrol boats.

Three surplus Type 23s were sold to Chile, and delivered between 2006 and 2008, which is the only other operator of the ship.

In the 2021 defence review it was announced that two Type 23s would be retired early to save money on the cost of the LIFEX programme, including fitting Sea Cepter missiles. HMS *Monmouth* was decommissioned in 2021 and HMS *Montrose* is to follow in 2023.

TYPE 23 ANTI-SUBMARINE WARFARE FRIGATE

Complement: 185 (accommodation for up to 205)

Displacement: 4,900 tons (4,800 long tons)

Length: 133m (436ft 4in)

Beam: 16.1m (52ft 10in)

Draught: 7.3m (23ft 11in)

Propulsion: Two × Rolls-Royce Marine Spey SM1C

Speed: In excess of 52 kph; (28kts)

Range: 14,000km; 9,000 miles)

Armament:

Anti-air missiles: One × 32-cell Sea Ceptor GWS 35 Vertical Launching System (VLS) canisters

Anti-submarine torpedoes: Two × twin Stingray torpedo tubes

Guns One × BAE 4.5in Mk 8 naval gun, two × 30mm DS30M Mk2 guns, or two × 30mm DS30B guns, two × Miniguns, four × 7.62mm General-Purpose Machine Guns

Aviation:

One × Wildcat HMA2 or Merlin HM2

Allied Frigates

New Sub Hunters

The last Oliver Hazard Perry-class frigates were retired in 2015, which left the United States Navy without a dedicated anti-submarine warship. This capability gap is being filled by FFG-62 or Constellation-class multi-mission guided-missile frigates (right). In April 2020, the US Navy announced that Fincantieri Marinette Marine had won the contract with a modified design based on the FREMM, designed by Naval Group and Fincantieri.

Under current plans the US Navy intends to buy 20 of the warships, and construction of the first of class, USS *Constellation*, began on August 21, 2022. She is expected to enter service in 2026. (US NAVY)

The FREMM Frégate Européenne Multi-Mission/Fregata Europea Multi-Missione) is Europe's multi-purpose frigate (left). It is a Franco-Italian family of multi-purpose vessels designed by France's Naval Group and Italy's Fincantieri. It come comes in a number of variants, including a dedicated anti-submarine version.

In France, the ship is known as the Aquitaine-class and eight have been built. The Italian variant is known as the Bergamini-class and ten are on the order books.

The lead ship of the class, FS *Aquitaine*, was commissioned in November 2012 by the French Navy. Italy has ordered six general purpose and four anti-submarine variants. France has ordered six anti-submarine variants and two air-defence ones. (FABIUS1975)

The F110 class, also known as the Bonifaz class, are a multi-purpose, anti-submarine class of Aegis combat system-fitted heavy frigates under construction for the Spanish Navy (right). The project is being co-developed by the Spanish Ministry of Defence and the state-owned company Navantia. Construction of the first ship, ESFS *Bonifaz* started in April 2022, and it is expected to be delivered in 2025.

The new frigates have a projected operational life of 40 years and are capable of operating with unmanned vehicles - aerial, surface, and sub-surface. (BUQUESDEGUERRA.COM)

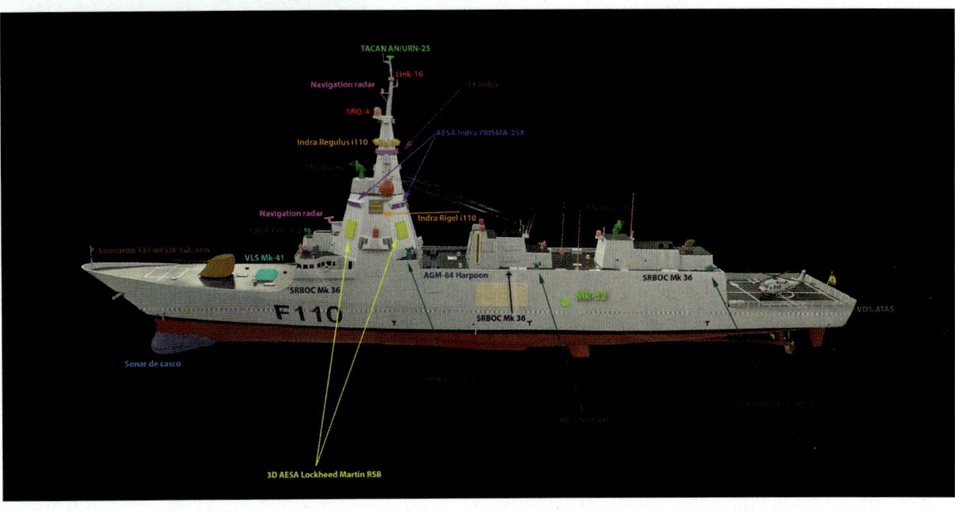

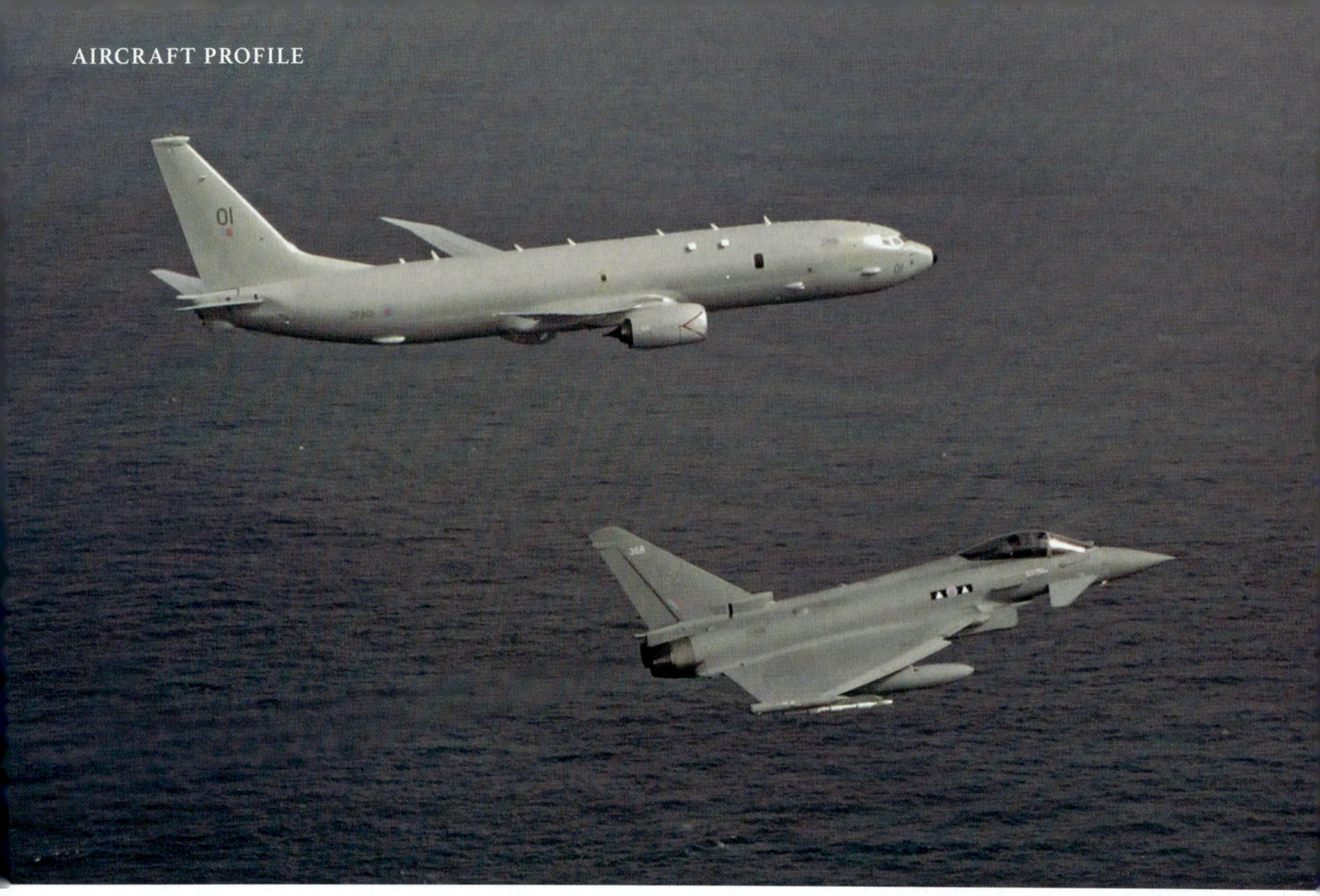

Poseidon at Work

The RAF's New Maritime Patrol Aircraft on Duty

ABOVE: RAF Lossiemouth is the hub for RAF operations over the North Atlantic. Poseidon and Typhoon units at the station are held at high readiness to react to Russian air and naval incursions into the UK's area of interest in North Atlantic. (MOD/CROWN COPYRIGHT)

With daily media headlines about aggressive Russian naval deployments, rising energy prices and allegations of sabotage against undersea gas pipelines it becomes easier to explain and justify why the Royal Air Force needs its £2.2bn fleet of nine Boeing Poseidon MRA1 maritime patrol aircraft.

That is the view of the commander of the RAF's first operational Poseidon unit, CXX Squadron, Wing Commander Ben Livesey. "The attack on the Nordstream gas pipeline in the Baltic Sea in 2022 showed the vulnerabilities of UK energy supplies," he said. "Ordinary people realise events like that affect them and their energy bills. The public can see it."

In 2022, the RAF Poseidon Force passed a key capability milestone, and it is now delivering a return on the British taxpayer's investment in resurrecting the UK's maritime patrol capability.

In the entrance to the Atlantic Building at RAF Lossiemouth there is a very large painting of an RAF Poseidon overflying a Russian nuclear-powered attack submarine. It is a statement of intent and leaves no one in any doubt about what Wing Commander Livesey and his crews are focused on.

The former Nimrod mission commander declared: "The Cold War isn't over. Since 24 February 2022 it has come back. Russia has credible [military] capability and is willing to use it. Russia is an aggressive power, and we need to be able to protect UK waters and our freedom of movement."

Livesey and his team do not doubt the scale of the task facing them. Russian submarines of the 21st century are of a different magnitude

RIGHT: All nine Poseidon MRA1 ordered in 2015 to restore the RAF's maritime patrol capability have been delivered to RAF Lossiemouth. (MOD/CROWN COPYRIGHT)

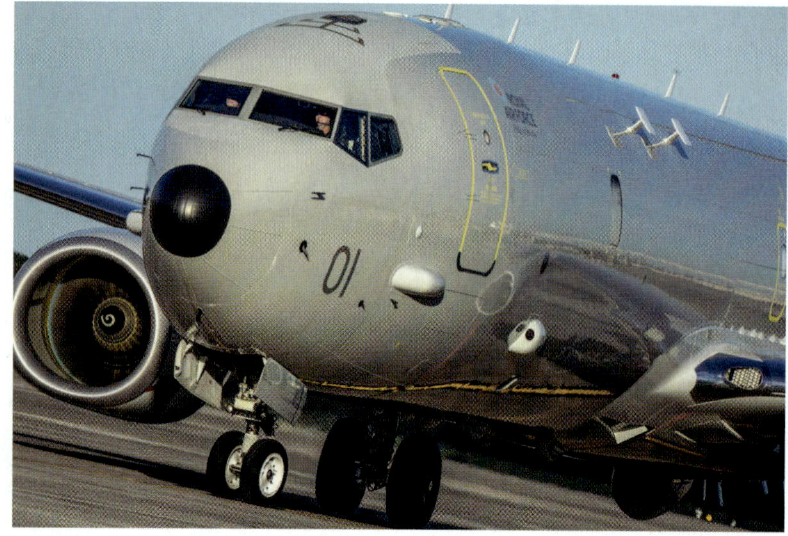

of capability compared to during the Cold War era before 1990. One of his colleagues described the Russian Yasen-class nuclear attack submarine, the RFS *Severdinsk*, as "one of best submarines in the world today."

As well as bringing their new aircraft and supporting systems into service after the first Poseidons were delivered to the UK in 2020, Livesey said that rebuilding the 'maritime ops' spirit and ethos across the RAF was also part of the effort to create a credible UK maritime patrol capability.

Livesey said that his Poseidon crews do not try to find Russia's submarine by themselves but integrate their operations with the Royal Navy and allied navies.

This has prompted a surge in demand for support from the RAF's Poseidons. "Everyone wants to use us - the insatiable appetite across defence for intelligence, surveillance and reconnaissance (ISR) has not abated," he said. "The challenge for me is educating people what the Poseidon can do. The danger is opening the flood gates to tasking. It could be a double-edged sword."

To meet that demand for tasking the RAF Poseidon fleet has rapidly grown since 2020 when initial operating capability was declared, with one aircraft and one crew available. On June 30, 2022, it achieved what was termed interim capability milestone (ICM), which means it was judged able to sustain continuous operations for an extended period, executing any of its six core tasks. The exact period is classified but is believed to be measured in days.

Livesey said core tasks were:

1. Anti-Submarine Warfare operations for Royal Navy against submerged targets
2. Anti surface warfare operations against surface vessels
3. Maritime counter terrorist operations
4. Search and Rescue (SAR) for submerged submarines
5. Surface SAR in co-operation with partners
6. Bespoke tasks for Air Command

Livesey revealed that his squadron had been activated on three occasions up to the middle of 2023, prompting them to launch "full rate effort," for the required period. Even when not activated for "full rate effort," three Poseidon crews are at varying degrees of readiness for short notice tasking, such as SAR missions or in reaction to a surprise incursion into British territorial waters by Russian vessels.

The next target for the RAF Poseidon fleet is to grow to full operating capability, or FOC, during 2024, which Livesey described as a "major hurdle." This required the Poseidon crews to operate at full rate effort for an extended period, including from a deployed location. »

LEFT: RAF Poseidon aircraft are now routinely dispatched to investigate suspicious naval activity across the North Atlantic region. (MOD/CROWN COPYRIGHT)

BELOW: The Poseidon MRA1 is based on the Boeing 737 airliner but the airframe has been reinforced to allow for prolonged operations at low level. (MOD/CROWN COPYRIGHT)

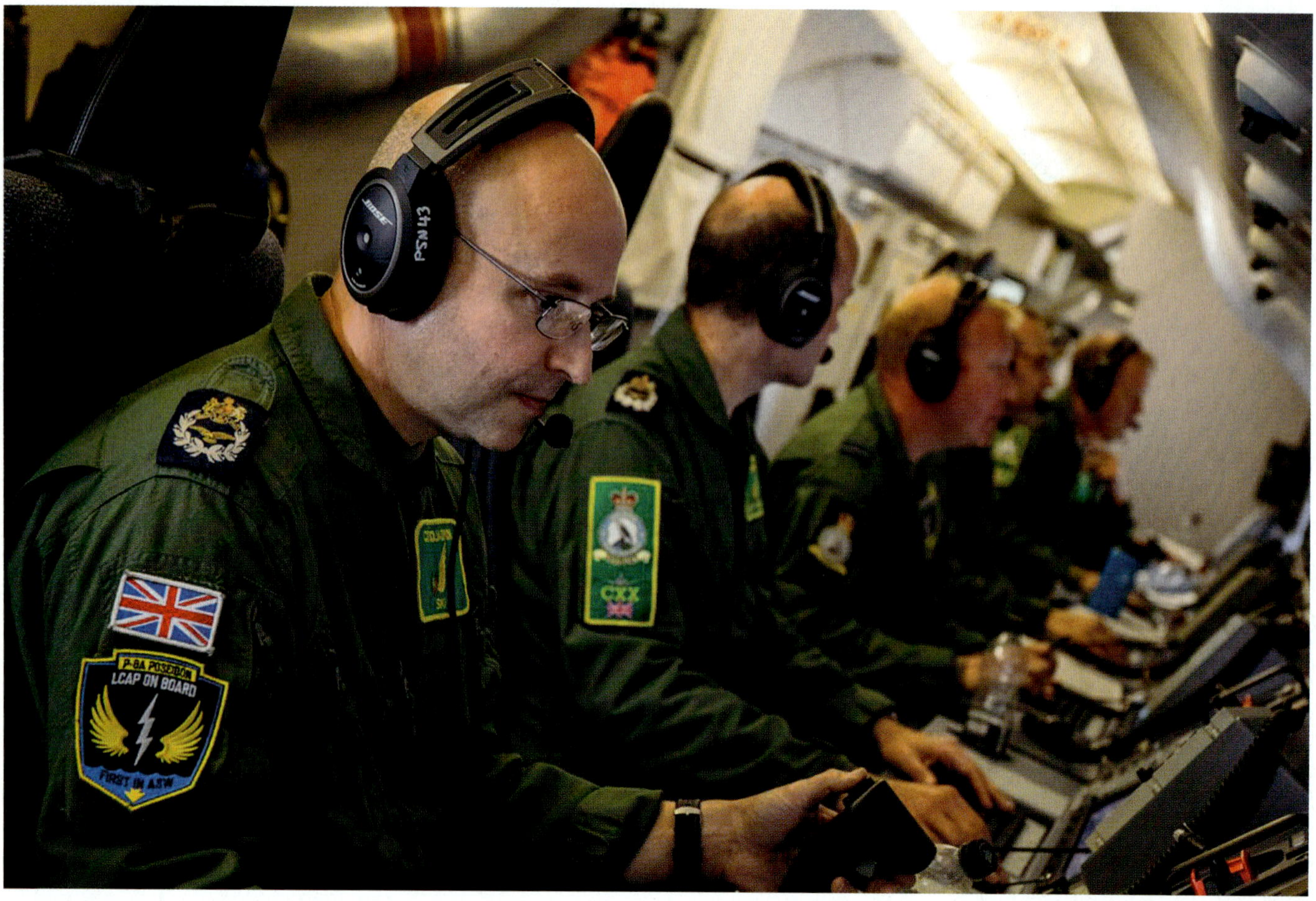

ABOVE: Mission crews on RAF Poseidon aircraft are a mix of officers and senior non-commissioned officers. Many have experience on the old Nimrod or have undertaken exchange training with allied maritime patrol units. (MOD/CROWN COPYRIGHT)

To meet the FOC target the Poseidon fleet has evolved since 2020. There are now three force elements, CXX and 201 Squadrons. which take on operational tasking. In September 2023, 42 (Torpedo Bomber) Squadron reformed, and it became the Poseidon operational conversion or training unit, as well as overseeing engineering and airworthiness of the aircraft. There is also a standards and evaluation team within 42 Squadron and a forward element from the RAF ISR test and evaluation unit, 56 Squadron, based at RAF Lossiemouth.

Building up the engineering and logistic support for the RAF Poseidon fleet operation has also taken place at a breakneck speed. All engineering activity is based in or around the Atlantic Building, which was completed in two years and opened in 2020 to coincide with the arrival of the first aircraft. The RAF works closely with Boeing Defence UK to sustain its Poseidons with around 200 company staff also working at RAF Lossiemouth in field service and maintenance roles.

"We are developing as a force and we need to get better," said Livesey.

RIGHT: 42 (Torpedo Bomber) Squadron reformed in September 2023 to take on the Poseidon operational conversion and engineering support role at RAF Lossiemouth. (MOD/CROWN COPYRIGHT)

"No one comes in at degree level at the start. Tracking submarines is difficult – the Russians have some of the best submarines in the world. We need to get crews up to the standard to take them on."

Geographic Focus

The focus of the RAF Poseidon fleet is still firmly on the North Atlantic and High North, with Livesey saying his aircraft routinely operated up to 1,000 miles from RAF Lossiemouth. The squadron has undertaken single aircraft deployments to the US Navy airbases at Keflavik in Iceland and Sigonella on Sicily for exercises.

The pace of activity within CXX Squadron is steadily increasing with Livesey saying that 40% to 60% of all sorties involve operational activity. This is helping to build the credibility of the RAF Poseidon fleet as it proves to UK defence, allies, and potential opponents that it can deliver, he said. "We have found every Russian submarine we have been tasked to find – we have a 100% detection and tracking rate," said Livesey. "If we deliver against task – that makes your force credible."

"To achieve an ASW task I have to detect, locate and classify a target to say I have found a submarine," he said. "We can do that by dropping an acoustic sonobuoy sensor into the water or with radar and electro-optical sensors."

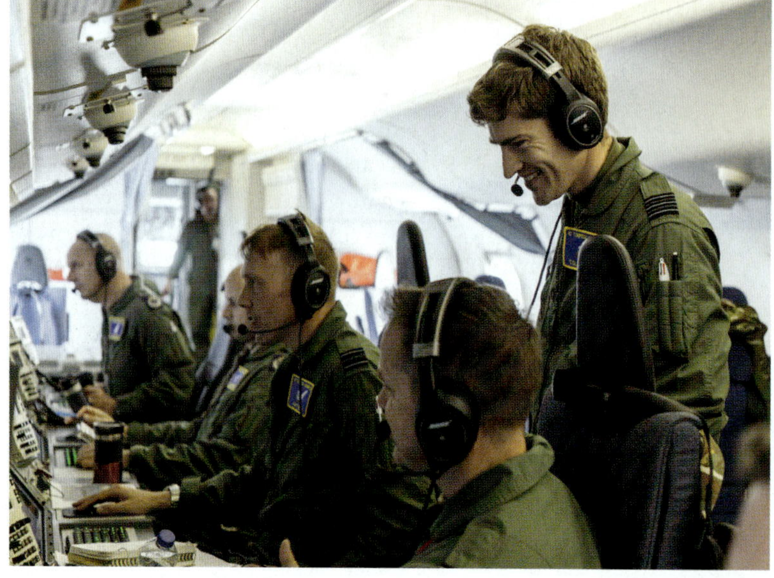

Tracking submerged submarines from the air is a complex and time-consuming exercise. It involves the dropping of fields of multiple sonobuoys to allow sonar returns to be triangulated by operators onboard the Poseidon. Water temperature and salinity can all impact on the performance of sonobuoys, which are also impacted by oceanic drift.

"It is hard to find and hard to keep hold of a submarine," said Livesey. "They are designed to be stealthy and if we find them, they want to slip away. If we detect them, they do their best to dodge detection."

When CXX Squadron is tasked over an extended period, the eight- to nine-hour long fuel endurance of the Poseidon means that aircraft crews have to swap over tasks in mid-submarine hunt, handing over control and monitoring of sonobuoy fields to other RAF or allied maritime patrol aircraft. "We have to hand over, aircraft to aircraft - UK or allied," said Livesey. "We operate within the coalition so can hand over assets. If we are tasked for seven days, then we need to be on task for seven days."

It is now routine for them to drop all, or nearly all, of their load of 129 sonobuoys during operational missions. They have experimented with flying with one or two additional crew members so they can be on hand to re-load the sonobuoy dispensers from storage

bays. This allows the mission crew, who would otherwise be required to do this task, to concentrate on monitoring their sensors and consoles.

The sonobuoys are complex sensors, including passive and active sonar variants, as well specialist versions to provide water condition information. The RAF currently buys its sonobuoys, via a Foreign Military Sales (FMS) contract with the US Navy's Air Systems Command (NAVAIR) and does not have an unlimited supply. Monitoring and managing their expenditure is a key issue for senior RAF officers in the Poseidon fleet. "Expending on sonobuoys is a judgement call when on task and a challenge for our chain

of command," said Livesey. "It is an issue deciding where to put resource."

Re-integration

The re-emergence of the RAF MPA capability after a 10-year gap has meant the branch has had to fit it into the service's current command and control architecture and establish new relationships with the Royal Navy and NATO's command structure. All these relationships are very different from in 1990 when the RAF had its own dedicated maritime patrol organisation, 18 Group, which was co-located with the Royal Navy's Fleet Headquarters at Northwood, outside London, and headed by a three-star officer.

Today, the Poseidon squadrons sit within the RAF Intelligence, »

ABOVE: Seven of the nine RAF Poseidon aircraft bear the names of famous people or places association with RAF Lossiemouth or RAF maritime patrol squadrons. Aircraft ZP803 is named *Terence Bulloch DSO* DFC**, after one of the most highly decorated Coastal Command pilots of World War Two. He was a founding member of re-formed 120 Squadron in 1941 and is credited with sinking three U-boats. He was awarded two Distinguished Service Orders and two Distinguished Flying Crosses.
(MOD/CROWN COPYRIGHT)

FAR LEFT: 201 Squadron is known as Guernsey's Own after its long association with the Channel Island. Poseidon ZP806 is named *Guernsey's Reply* after a World War Two Spitfire flown by a native who escaped the island ahead of its occupation by the Germans in 1940 and joined the RAF to fight to liberate the only occupied British territory.
(MOD/CROWN COPYRIGHT)

LEFT: CXX Squadron has long tradition as a maritime patrol unit stretching back to 1941 when it was reformed to fly Consolidated B-24 Liberators during the Battle of the Atlantic. It was credited with sinking 14 U-boats outright and with a share in sinking three more, plus eight damaged. The squadron personnel won three Distinguished Service Orders and one bar, two Military Crosses, one Military Medal and 27 Distinguished Flying Cross and two bars.
(MOD/CROWN COPYRIGHT)

ABOVE: RAF Poseidons are on 24 hour standby at RAF Lossiemouth to respond to maritime incursions into UK waters and ships in distress. (TIM RIPLEY)

Surveillance, Targeting, Acquisition and Reconnaissance (ISTAR) Force, which is in turn part of the RAF's 1 Group.

The RAF has now moved to what is known as the global air component concept, with all operational tasking, either in the UK or overseas, controlled and directed by the headquarters of 11 Group at RAF High Wycombe in Buckinghamshire. Outside agencies – from the UK military, UK government department, NATO, or allied nations – request air support from No 11 Group and it then tasks CXX or 201 Squadron.

Once on task, individual Poseidon aircraft operate under the tactical control of the Royal Navy-led maritime air operations centre, or MAOP, at Northwood or naval flag commands at sea, such as a Royal Navy carrier strike group battle staff.

Wing Commander Adam Smolak, who heads up 201 Squadron, described the Poseidon as a "world beating aircraft" and "state-of-the art."

RIGHT: An RAF Poseidon of 201 Squadron was scrambled in November 2023 to assist a yacht in trouble in the North Atlantic. The crew flew overwatch above the stricken yacht, *Heidi,* which had lost its masts in a storm and then directed the tanker *Green Azure* to rescue the yacht's captain. (MOD/CROWN COPYRIGHT)

"It is very reliable - we have not lost aircraft sorties due to aircraft serviceability," he said. "The crew like to fly it."

Smolak was keen dispel the impression it is a converted airliner that could not operate at low level in tactical situations. "Poseidon is not designed as a 737," he said. "It is designed as a maritime patrol aircraft, with thicker skin, a weapons bay, and a strengthened wing spar. It is manoeuvrable and stable; we fly it at 200 feet."

"It is early days," said Smolak, "we are growing, and we can see growing demand. Over the next 10 years we will be protecting UK waters, conducting deployed operations, and protecting the Royal Navy carriers with wide area maritime surveillance. We envisage we will have world-wide employment."

However, many in the RAF Poseidon community stress that they are not just re-creating the old Nimrod force. The world of underwater warfare technology has changed in the 30 years since the Nimrod hunted down Soviet submarines. The current Russian submarine fleet may well be considerably smaller than its Soviet predecessors, but its boats are now far quieter and to hunt them down needs highly trained operators with state-of-the-art equipment.

BELOW: In November 2023, the Ministry of Defence announced the launch of a project to integrate the UK's Stingray homing torpedo onto the RAF Poseidon MRA1s. This will augment the US-supplied Mark 54 homing torpedoes currently used. (MOD/CROWN COPYRIGHT)

Future Sub Hunters

The Underwater Battle in the 21st Century

ABOVE: The RAF is looking to use its new Protector unmanned aerial vehicles to deliver sonobuoys to help expand the coverage of its anti-submarine force. (MOD/CROWN COPYRIGHT)

Underwater warfare is changing rapidly thanks to the development of robot vessels and artificial intelligence (AI) technology. This is leading to major changes to how submarines are built and operate. This in turn will require a significant change in how they are hunted down and killed. A revolution in naval warfare is underway and it is not yet clear where it will end.

After Russia's invasion of Ukraine in February 2022, the Black Sea became a venue for the first naval conflict involving the widespread use of maritime drones. Remotely controlled speed boats, packed with explosives, were used by the Ukrainians to strike at Russian warships, harbours, and the Kerch Bridge.

The potential for robot technology has already been recognised by several other navies and they launched projects to incorporate it in underwater vessels. The idea is to create swarms of 'smart' underwater drones that can overwhelm enemy defences. These go beyond just being a big salvo of homing torpedoes. Concepts under development include drones that can operate over thousands of kilometres range, attack from multiple directions, or loiter on the sea bed to wait for a suitable target to appear.

The most ambitious of these new super drones is Russia's Poseidon underwater drone, previously called the Status-6 and which NATO calls the Kanyon. Unveiled in 2015, Russia's President Vladmir Putin bills the Poseidon as a nuclear-powered unmanned underwater vehicle that can carry both conventional and nuclear warheads. He said it would be capable of destroying enemy infrastructural facilities, aircraft carrier groups, and other large coastal targets. It is reported to have a range of more than 6,000 kilometres and being able to carry a two megaton thermo-nuclear warhead.

Unsurprisingly, the Russians have released few details of the weapon. It is still undergoing tests, and little is known about how it is performing. From the few images that have been published it is more than 20 metres long and looks like a giant torpedo. It is so big that the Russian navy has had to develop a special submarine to carry it, the Project 09852 submarine RFS *Belgorod,* which entered service with the Northern Fleet in 2022. The submarine has special extra-large weapon tubes in its bows to accommodate several Poseidons.

RIGHT: The US Navy's P-8 Poseidon force has carried out training exercises involving US Air Force MQ-9A Reaper unmanned aerial vehicles in the Pacific, culminating in a live fire exercise that sank the decommissioned ex-USS *Rodney M. Davis*. (US AIR FORCE)

ABOVE: The RFS *Belgorod* was moved out of the submarine assembly hall at the SEVMASH yard at Severodvinsk in 2019. She is destined to be a 'mother-ship' for a range of underwater vehicles. (TASS)

LEFT: The Harpsichord-2P-PM Unmanned Underwater Vehicle (UUV) is expected to be carried by the RFS *Belgorod*. These UUVs carry an array of sonars including side-scanning and are able to map the sea floor in great detail and locate items such as wreckage and sensor arrays. (TASS)

If the Poseidon works as advertised, then it has the potential to be able to strike at targets on the west coast of the United States of America from a launch point near to Iceland. A multi-pronged attack by many Poseidons would pose huge challenges for allied underwater defences. Unmanned drones can potentially operate at greater depth than crewed submarines, making them harder to find and track. And this trait would be further enhanced by the nuclear power plant of the Poseidon which could also be significantly quieter that those used in conventional submarines.

Swarm Technology

To defend against these new types of underwater threats, allied navies are having to think again about how they conduct anti-submarine warfare. In future, allied submarines, frigates, and maritime patrol aircraft will have to become hubs to launch and control counter-swarms of defensive underwater drones.

One concept under consideration by several navies envisages equipping submarines and warships with their own short range drone swarms. These would be a sort of combined sonobuoy/homing torpedo that

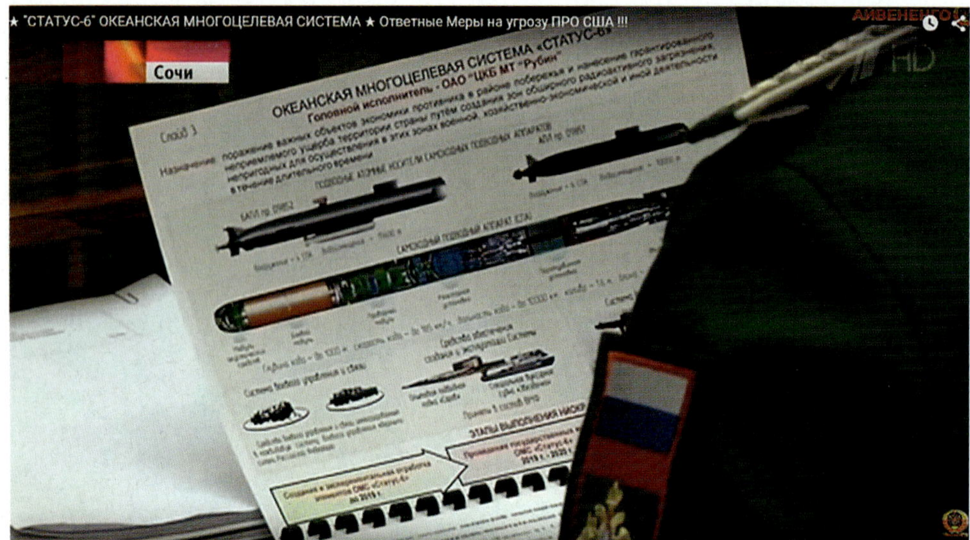

ABOVE: Some of the first details of the Ocean Multipurpose System Status-6, or Poseidon, nuclear torpedo emerged in 2016 via reports on the Russian state-owned-TV Channel One. (CHANNEL ONE)

BELOW: In February 2019, the US Navy awarded Boeing a $43m contract to build four Orca experimental Extra Large Unmanned Undersea Vehicles (XLUUVs). They are intended to carry out long range missions to monitor huge areas of ocean. (BOEING)

could be sown in a large pattern around a warships or submarine to hunt for enemy submarines or even rival drone swarms. This would turn submarines into control hubs operating over hundreds of kilometres range. The drones would be launched from conventional torpedo tubes or from a 'moon pool' or docks under the hull of a submarine.

Warships would also be an able to fire off short range drones from deck mounted rapid launchers. For longer range employment, aerial drones could be used to drop underwater drones in their target areas. These drones could be far cheaper and easier to use than manned helicopters, allowing warships to carry far more of them.

Russia's Poseidon is the nightmare scenario for allied underwater defenders, requiring rapid improvement in wide ocean surveillance capabilities. The US Navy and Royal Navy are both working to develop what are called extra-large unmanned underwater vehicles, or XLUUV. The experimental British version is dubbed Project Manta, and a prototype has been built to test if it is possible for a drone to be able to cruise for three months underwater, some 3,000 nautical miles from its launch point. The idea behind the Manta is to use them to patrol deep under the North Atlantic for months at a time to give early warning of the approach of Russian submarines or drones.

These concepts all point to future anti-submarine warfare being very different from today. The idea of big warships, submarines and maritime patrol aircraft duelling with each other could be a thing of the past. In future, swarms of drones will bear the brunt of the battle to control the underwater domain. The big and expensive manned platforms will be able to step back and become control hubs. To destroy a warship or submarine will require swarms of drones to defeat their enemy's drone swarm.

Sub-hunting has come a long way from the days of RAF Coastal Command Catalina flying boat pilots winning the Victoria Cross for pressing home attacks on surfaced U-boats during the Battle of the Atlantic. However, the essential truth of anti-submarine warfare remains unchanged. It remains a duel for technological superiority. The move to underwater drones has the potential to render the current generation of submarines obsolete, or at least make them highly vulnerable. How the reaction/counter reaction moves play out remains to be seen but it seems that the 'great duel' has moved on.

While the potential for drones in underwater warfare is immense, this technological nirvana has not yet been reached. For many years to come, the crews of submarines, frigates, helicopters, and patrol aircraft will still be needed to risk their lives under, on, or above the world's oceans.